YOUTH COMPREHENSIVE RISK ASSESSMENT

Youth Comprehensive Risk Assessment: A Clinically Tested Approach for Helping Professionals presents a complete youth risk assessment and treatment program based on Dr. Ken Coll's 20 plus years of research on assessing and treating at-risk youth. In this book, helping professionals will find not only a wide range of succinct and easy-to-use assessments, but also proven helpful, highly specific approaches and treatment strategies. Case studies and intervention techniques show professionals—from therapists and social workers to teachers and nurses—how they can help struggling youth find motivation to work on their concerns. This book also offers professionals a menu of assessment surveys and action strategies so that they can develop a plan that best fits the needs of particular youth and their families.

Kenneth M. Coll, PhD, is a professor in counseling at the University of Nevada, Reno. He is a Licensed Professional Counselor (clinical), Master Addictions Counselor, and has been awarded Researcher of the Year at two different universities. He also has recently served on the Governor's Behavioral Health Transformation Task Force.

YOUTH COMPREHENSIVE RISK ASSESSMENT

A Clinically Tested Approach for Helping Professionals

Kenneth M. Coll

Routledge
Taylor & Francis Group

NEW YORK AND LONDON

First published 2017
by Routledge
711 Third Avenue, New York, NY 10017

and by Routledge
2 Park Square, Milton Park, Abingdon, Oxon, OX14 4RN

Routledge is an imprint of the Taylor & Francis Group, an informa business

© 2017 Taylor & Francis

The right of Kenneth M. Coll to be identified as author of this work has been asserted by him in accordance with sections 77 and 78 of the Copyright, Designs and Patents Act 1988.

Library of Congress Cataloging in Publication Data
Names: Coll, Kenneth M., author.
Title: Youth comprehensive risk assessment : a clinically tested approach for helping professionals / by Kenneth M. Coll.
Description: 1 Edition. | New York : Routledge, 2017.
Includes bibliographical references and index.
Identifiers: LCCN 2016048526 | ISBN 9781138945531 (hbk. :alk. paper) | ISBN 9781138945517 (pbk. : alk. paper) | ISBN 9781315671260 (ebook)
Subjects: LCSH: Risk-taking (Psychology) | Behavior therapy for teenagers.
Classification: LCC BF637.R57 C65 2017 DDC 153.8/3–dc23
LC record available at https://lccn.loc.gov/2016048526

ISBN: 978-1-138-94553-1 (hbk)
ISBN: 978-1-138-94551-7 (pbk)
ISBN: 978-1-315-67126-0 (ebk)

Typeset in Baskerville
by Wearset Ltd, Boldon, Tyne and Wear

To my wife, Brenda, my love and my inspiration

CONTENTS

PREFACE

Perhaps the most common model for working with youth today is to provide the education and resources *before* the youth engages in high-risk behaviors, essentially—the public health and prevention approach. Prevention models are powerful tools, and should over time reduce the suffering of youth and minimize the cost of tertiary treatment. As often noted, if we teach someone to fish upstream, society will not need to provide them with fish downstream. Given the popularity of prevention, we may overlook a larger truth—that a substantial and alarming proportion of today's youth are already downriver.

Downriver youth have rich strengths, but in their rapid descent downstream they are often pounded by collisions with substance abuse, domestic violence, academic failure, and dysfunctional family systems.

This book is dedicated to downriver youth and their families and to the professionals who work downriver.

ACKNOWLEDGMENTS

This book was made possible by a number of important collaborations that have been a very meaningful and jubilant part of my life. I have been very fortunate to work with two outstanding scholars, Jerry Juhnke and Roger Stewart; and excellent practitioners, including John Butgereit, Nicole Hauser, Mike Cutler, and Robin Hass. I have also been graced in my 30-year collaboration with Patti Thobro, a clinician extraordinaire, good friend, and organizational wizard!

I have worked with an excellent group of students over the years, which has resulted in important related collaborations, including Stephanie Powell, Ann Trotter, Nick Barclay, Margaret Sass, Megan Smith Robinson, and Megan Keller.

Most importantly, my wife, Brenda, has provided love, friendship, support, and wonderful conceptualization and organization. She is an outstanding scholar in her own right and has provided countless suggestions and creativity to this work of over 25 years. I have learned a lot from her both in our joint writing and in the applicability of her own research to mine.

Let me finally acknowledge every youth I have encountered who has worked bravely and diligently to make their lives better, even with seemingly insurmountable odds against them. They are truly the heroes of these stories within.

INTRODUCTION

From Struggling to Thriving Youth

The YCRA, A Clinically Tested Approach for Helping Professionals presents a complete youth risk assessment and treatment program based on my 20 plus years of research and collaboration. I've been working mostly with an award-winning child and adolescent treatment facility and have also set up assessment systems and consulted with other adolescent agencies working with hard-to-reach youth. In this book, helping professionals will find not only a wide range of succinct and easy-to-use assessments, but also proven helpful, highly specific approaches and treatment strategies.

In long-term research with over 700 youth, I discovered certain key factors that engage youth to become more resilient. These data-based findings, which are explained here in clear, comprehensible language, form the basis of my youth comprehensive risk assessment and application (YCRA). This approach has two goals: 1) implementing individualized and comprehensive assessment, and 2) teaching youth and their families to develop a unique set of protective or buffering factors that promote thriving.

I will show how, as helping professionals, you can help struggling youth find motivation to work on their concerns. I will give helping professionals the tools to teach youth and their families fundamental skills, and to develop and strengthen their resiliency. Action strategies are offered, and you can choose among the assessment tools and strategies that best fit the needs of particular youth and their families you may be working with, whatever your clientele's specific challenges.

What You Can Expect From This Book

You may have picked this book because you want more tools for your toolbox. Perhaps you are toying with the idea of working more with adolescents. You may want to pursue similar research and practice in working with difficult-to-help youth. Or you may just want to learn more about adolescents, and what helps them. In any of these cases, this book can help.

This book describes the evolution of the YCRA by first describing its major components and effective interventions, then by describing "putting it all together" into a dynamic, inclusive assessment tool, and finally describing outcome-based evidence of wide-ranging strategies and interventions that provide validation for the YCRA and really work.

As illustrated, Part I describes the important components that make up the YCRA, including asset building, psychosocial development, family engagement, and behavioral issues. I will show you how to apply these concepts and their accompanying best practice interventions to youth in need.

In Part II, I describe the trajectory and maturation of the YCRA approach and introduce other useful clinician and client individualized assessments. I will also use an illustrative example for *putting the assessments all together* in a valuable way and discuss *key trends and results* discovered in over 700 cases.

Part III delves more deeply into contextual issues of *applications and interventions* discussed in Part I and tackles the *challenge of motivation and readiness for change* strategies per the YCRA assessment results (see YCRA and applications illustration below). Particular *challenges for ethnically diverse and historically oppressed youth* are also included, using a case example to illustrate pertinent practical applications. Finally, the importance of *psychopharmacology* as well as *helping professional issues* concerning burnout, wellness, and workplace dilemmas conclude this book.

I hope that the examples I relate in this book will help you immediately apply what you have learned.

In summary, this book shares with you the shortcuts and best practices I have learned over the last 20 plus years. I want you to succeed in your professional pursuits and help youth in the best ways possible. So join me as I guide you through the sometimes frustrating but ultimately rewarding work in helping at-risk youth to overcome their challenges and thrive. I think you will enjoy the journey.

Part I

Asset building = Chapter 1
Psychosocial development = Chapter 2
Family engagement = Chapter 3
Behavioral issues = Chapter 4

Part II

Youth comprehensive risk assessment = Chapter 5

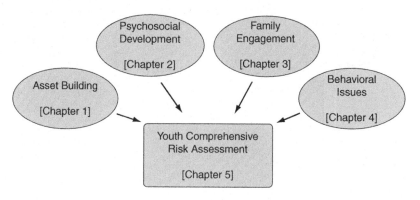

Part III

Motivation and readiness for change applications = Chapter 6
Challenges for ethnically diverse and historically oppressed
youth = Chapter 7
Psychopharmacology = Chapter 8
Helping professional issues = Chapter 9

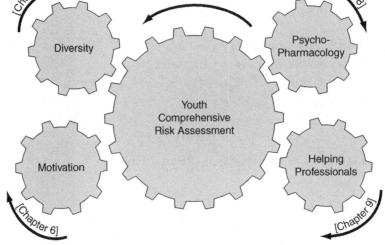

PART I
THE COMPONENTS

1

RISK, RESILIENCY, AND ASSET BUILDING

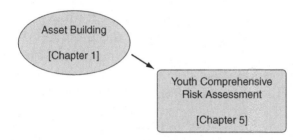

Key Learning Concepts
- Risk
- Resiliency
- Application of the Asset Checklist (key YCRA component)
- Commonly reported high and low assets
- Strategies and interventions that work
- An example of a school-based asset intervention

Jason is a gawky and talkative 16-year-old with tremendous obstacles to deal with. He has had one recent suicide attempt, and he was just charged with assault for fighting. He is currently a grade behind in school and has frequent angry outbursts. He began drinking and smoking marijuana at age 13. He has been living with his grandmother for the last four years. His father is in prison and he has had no contact with his mother for the last 10 years.

These facts about Jason sound pretty grim, don't they? All too often we stop here and try to help as best we can, focusing on decreasing these behaviors. However, with that approach, we are missing a great deal on painting the overall picture of who Jason is, which is an essential component of understanding what he needs and what the best approach is to work with him.

Jason turns out to be a gifted athlete, excelling in soccer and football. In spite of being a year behind in school, his teachers have noticed his genuine talents and interest in science. He makes friends easily and is a loyal friend back. It pains him to think his behavior has disappointed and hurt his grandmother, someone he cares deeply about, and she for him.

It is true that we often focus on the problems, the deficits. But aren't a youth's strengths more important? Isn't the more balanced question, how do we help Jason grow his strengths and reduce his obstacles, self-imposed or otherwise?

Risk and Resiliency

Risk

We know a great deal about the factors that contribute to risky behaviors in adolescence. The research literature (American Academy of Child and Adolescent Psychiatry Council, 2010; Duke, Borowsky, Pettingell, & McMorris, 2011; Subramaniam, Lewis, Stitzer, & Fishman, 2004) consistently reports the following factors:

- high levels of alcohol and other drug (AOD) abuse
- lack of parent–child closeness
- family conflict
- beliefs and attitudes favorable to criminality
- early childhood aggressiveness, antisocial behavior, and poor peer acceptance.

Additionally, we know that high-risk behavior in adolescents has long been associated with certain societal ills (Huizinga, Loeber, Thornberry, & Cothern, 2000; Hawkins et al., 2000), such as:

- lower socioeconomic status (i.e., poverty)
- easy access to alcohol and other drugs and family splintering
- co-occurring AOD abuse and mental health problems.

Common clinical practice is to provide broad-based problem-focused assessment, with heavy reliance on clinical judgment without any room for what youths and their families perceive as their assets or strengths.

Resiliency

In fact, like Jason, despite extremely debilitating environmental, family, and personal experiences, many young people can develop impressive and reliant personal strengths. Indeed, a typical "troubled" adolescent like Jason often shows remarkable signs of what is called "resiliency," defined as a sustaining competence under stress and an ability to adapt and function with success despite chronic stress and adversity (McWhirter, McWhirter, McWhirter, & McWhirter, 2007).

So using the metaphor of a see saw, an often missed truism is that if we can intervene on the strengths' side—help a youth increase personal resilience or assets—we will also markedly help reduce risk factors.

The Wonderful World of Assets

Let's now work with Jason to assess his assets per the Search Institute's Asset Checklist, a thoroughly researched assessment tool that provides much evidence and proof that the more assets one can have, the more functional and successful one will be.

An Asset Checklist

Many people find it helpful to use a simple checklist to reflect on the assets young people experience. This checklist simplifies a youth's strengths to help prompt conversation and ideas. NOTE: This checklist is neither intended nor appropriate as a scientific or accurate measurement of developmental assets.

Jason: *Answer each question with T (True) or F (False)*

EXTERNAL ASSETS
Support

T   F

X ___ 1. I receive high levels of support from family members.

X ___ 2. I can go to my parent(s) or guardian(s) for advice and support and have frequent, in-depth conversations with them.

___ ___ 3. I know some non-parent adults I can go to for advice and support.

___ ___ 4. My neighbors encourage and support me.

___ ___ 5. My school provides a caring, encouraging environment.

___ ___ 6. My parent(s) or guardian(s) help me succeed in school.

Empowerment

T   F

___ ___ 7. I feel valued by adults in my community.

___ ___ 8. I am given useful roles in my community.

___ ___ 9. I serve in the community one hour or more a week.

X ___ 10. I feel safe at home, at school, and in the neighborhood.

Boundaries and Expectations

T   F

X ___ 11. My family sets standards for appropriate conduct and monitors my whereabouts.

_X_ ___ 12. My school has clear rules and consequences for behavior.

___ ___ 13. Neighbors take responsibility for monitoring my behavior.

___ ___ 14. Parent(s) and other adults model positive, responsible behavior.

___ ___ 15. My best friends model responsible behavior.

___ ___ 16. My parent(s)/guardian(s) and teachers encourage me to do well.

Constructive Use of Time

T   *F*

___ ___ 17. I spend three hours or more each week in lessons or practice music, theater, or other arts.

___ ___ 18. I spend three hours or more each week in school or community sports, clubs, or organizations.

___ ___ 19. I spend one hour or more each week in religious services or participating in spiritual activities.

___ ___ 20. I go out with friends "with nothing special to do" two or fewer nights each week.

INTERNAL ASSETS

Commitment to Learning

T   *F*

_X_ ___ 21. I want to do well in school.

___ ___ 22. I am actively engaged in learning.

___ ___ 23. I do an hour or more of homework each school day.

_X_ ___ 24. I care about school.

___ ___ 25. I read for pleasure three or more hours each week.

Positive Values

T   *F*

_X_ ___ 26. I believe it is really important to help other people.

_X_ ___ 27. I want to help promote equality and reduce hunger.

_X_ ___ 28. I can stand up for what I believe.

___ ___ 29. I tell the truth even when it's not easy.

___ ___ 30. I can accept and take personal responsibility.

___ ___ 31. I believe it is important not to be sexually active or to use alcohol or other drugs.

Social Competencies

T   F

___   ___   32. I am good at planning ahead and making decisions.

_X_   ___   33. I am good at making and keeping friends, cultural/ racial/ethnic backgrounds.

___   ___   35. I can resist negative peer pressure and dangerous situations.

_X_   ___   36. I try to resolve conflict nonviolently.

Positive Identity

T   F

_X_   ___   37. I believe I have control over many things that happen to me.

___   ___   38. I feel good about myself.

___   ___   39. I believe life has a purpose.

_X_   ___   40. I am optimistic about my future.

Note: Unanswered questions = FALSE

Jason identified some important assets that were verified by his grandmother, teachers, and the helping professional working with him. However, there are a number of potential assets "left on the table." It is generally accepted that youth who perceive only having 20 or fewer assets tend to struggle (Search Institute, 2015). That is the challenge for Jason and those helping him; how do we help Jason increase his number of assets?

Summary of Jason's Results

For *external assets* (assets Jason may be able to get from the world around him), he perceives strong support from his grandmother, but he does not feel support from his neighborhood and school, and seeks more support to help him be successful in school. While Jason feels safe at home, he is not engaged in his community, nor does he feel valued by it.

Although he sees clear boundaries and expectations from his grandmother and school, his friends do not model responsible behavior, and adult role models are lacking. He also does not see himself as getting much encouragement to do well in school and he does not use his time constructively.

Using the Asset Checklist to Shape Resiliency With External Assets

- Jason's answers here point to school and community engagement as key themes in all areas of external assets.
  - Research (Hawkins et al., 2000) indicates that school engagement occurs when students make a psychological investment in learning. They try hard to learn, and take pride in success. Youth community engagement typically means meaningful participation and sustained involvement in activities focused outside of self and invested in a community (including school).
  - The following are some tried and true tips for what teachers and school counselors can do to help Jason, gleaned from consensus of research studies (Huizinga et al., 2000):
    - Help him in practical matters, such as specific school work, school socialization (such as sports, clubs).
    - Acknowledge and normalize his challenges and problems.
    - Encourage his involvement in cooperative learning at school, and perhaps provide assertiveness training.
    - Recognize and share with Jason similar problems you have encountered.
    - Encourage his involvement in active classroom instruction, emphasize interactive teaching and cooperative learning, use tutoring as needed.
    - Identify Jason's positive behaviors, focus on specific deeds, use the language of encouragement, and focus on what he is good at and interested in.
    - Create pro-social ways to help Jason express interests by using a sound career guidance process.

- Coach Jason's grandmother to express concern while setting firm limits about school performance and activities.

With these approaches and interventions, all external assets, especially constructive use of time, will improve as well. For example, we already knew Jason was good at and interested in sports, but what we did not know until we talked with him about his assets was that he carried a passion for playing the saxophone. In his brief time playing in middle school he not only excelled but carried the school-borrowed sax everywhere and practiced any chance he got. He had not told anyone about this interest because he did not see any way he could continue after he got in trouble, and did not think he deserved to. Weekly lessons were immediately provided, and constructive use of time as well as his commitment to learning, like his playing, began to soar.

Using the Asset Checklist to Shape Resiliency With Internal Assets

For *internal assets* (assets that can come from within Jason), he perceives that he has positive values, especially with helping others, but does not see that he has much going in social competencies, commitment to learning, or positive identity. One might say that Jason feels very discouraged.

- Jason's answers specify that commitment to learning and social competencies may be key here. For example, even though he desires to help others, he is not sure he has anything much to offer.
  - Research evidence (Coll, Sass, Freeman, Thobro, & Hauser, 2013) shows that youth need a commitment to the lasting importance of learning and a belief in their own abilities to do so. Young people also need social competencies, which are the skills to build positive relationships, to put their values into action and cope with new situations.

- ○ Here are tips for what parents, teachers, and school counselors can do; again gleaned from numerous research studies:
  - Know that your beliefs about Jason affect his confidence and ability to learn.
  - Read for pleasure, because Jason will too if he sees you doing so.
  - Encourage Jason to deeply explore all options available to him in school. He may not be aware of interesting opportunities, like ski club, debate team, karate club.
  - Include Jason in discussions and decisions about his life whenever possible.
  - Help Jason connect to opportunities to learn and develop skills with responsible peers and adults, like school activities (see above).
  - Celebrate and model diversity for Jason.
  - Give Jason opportunities to develop more confidence and competence—for example, taking responsibility to prepare a meal.
  - Teach Jason the importance of choices and consequences to those choices whenever possible.

Similar to the process for increasing external assets, approaches and interventions targeted at commitment to learning and social competencies will result in positive values and identity and increased internal assets. For example, we discovered Jason's thirst for helping others during this exercise. He was especially enthusiastic about helping younger children who had been victims of physical violence or had witnessed it, given that he could relate to them with his own experience. We were able to connect him with a local agency where he began to read and teach music and soccer to first to third grade children staying at a domestic shelter. Again, his grades climbed, angry outbursts diminished, and he began speaking and acting like he valued himself and had a purpose in life.

Note: In the over 700 Asset Checklists I have analyzed, the two consistently highest reported assets tend to be *Positive Values* and *Family Support*. The two overwhelmingly lowest asset themes regularly are *Constructive Use of Time* and *Commitment to Learning*.

Sample Report with "At-Risk" Youth and "Non-at-Risk" Youth:
How Asset Building Works

I recently had the good fortune to work with a dedicated group of high school faculty. They were deeply concerned about some of their students (mostly freshmen and sophomores) who neither seemed engaged nor were performing academically well. We were able to set up an experiment in which we exposed those students to "heavy doses" of cooperative learning and used an ongoing checklist to incorporate the previously mentioned tips for one full semester:

- We established group goals. Before beginning an assignment, goals and objectives were defined.
- We used some simple group facilitation guidelines to frame the activities (see TeachThought.com). For example:
  - We kept the groups midsized (moderate size group of 4–5 is ideal).
  - We built trust and promoted open communication by dealing with emotional issues that arose immediately and any interpersonal problems before moving on. Assignments encouraged team members to explain concepts thoroughly to each other.
  - We created pre-tests and post-tests, with the Asset Checklist as one example. An assessment gives the team a goal.
  - We allowed groups to reduce anxiety—for example, use of appropriate humor and creating a more relaxed learning atmosphere that allows for positive learning experiences. We allowed groups to use some stress-reducing strategies as long as they stayed on task.
  - We used real-world problems.

- o Experts suggest that project-based learning using open-ended questions can be very engaging. Rather than spending a lot of time designing an artificial scenario, use inspiration from everyday problems. Real-world problems can be used to facilitate project-based learning and often have the right scope for collaborative learning.
- We rotated groups so students had a chance to learn from others.
- We used scaffolding as students began to understand concepts. At the beginning of a project, we gave more direction than at the end, allowing groups to grow in responsibility as times goes on. In your classroom, this may mean allowing teams to develop their own topics or products as time goes on.
- We included different types of learning scenarios, including laboratory work, study teams, debates, writing projects, problem solving, and collaborative writing.
- We allowed some individual time to write notes before the groups began to combat "group think."

The results far surpassed our expectations. Not only did the "at-risk" group make drastic improvements in turning "false assets" to "true assets," their behavior changed markedly as evidenced in significantly higher Grade Point Averages (GPAs), and lower absences and detentions. See Table 1.1.

Documented record reviews—at-risk group:

- GPA increased +0.5 average (from 2.0 in Fall semester to 2.5).
- Absences reduced –4 average (from 12 days in Fall semester to 8 days).
- Behavioral problems (detention) reduced –6 average (from 15 detentions in Fall semester to 9 detentions).

Comparison group: no changes.

Table 1.1 Asset summary report (pre/post, one semester)

Class	
At-risk group	N = 51 (defined as: poor academic performance; absences; behavioral problems) Avg. age = 14.5, 40% female; 60% male
Comparison group (c)	N = 102 Avg. age = 14.8, 42% female; 60% male

Asset construct	Definition	Pre-survey		Post-survey	
		% True	% False	% True	% False
Support	Explores how much a student perceives support from family, neighbors, school. Results = 10% improvement in this area for at-risk youth, especially in receiving support from three or more non-parent adults. Minimum improvement in comparison group.	65%	35%	75%	25%
		80% (c)	20% (c)	83% (c)	17% (c)
Empowerment	Measures the sense of empowerment youth perceive about the community. Results = 18% improvement for at-risk youth, especially in believing young people are given useful roles. Minimum improvement in comparison group.	50%	50%	68%	32%
		70% (c)	30% (c)	75% (c)	25% (c)

Boundaries and expectations	Measures the amount of clear rules and consequences provided to the youth. Results = little improvement in this area for both groups.	71% 81% (c)	29% 19% (c)	75% 82% (c)	25% 18% (c)
Constructive use of time	Measures constructive use of time in activities. Results = 20% improvement for at-risk youth, especially in activities (e.g., art, sports, clubs). Minimum improvement in comparison group.	35% 77% (c)	65% 23% (c)	55% 79% (c)	45% 21% (c)
Commitment to learning	Measures motivation and engagement in school. Results = 16% improvement for at-risk youth, especially in homework and reading. Minimum improvement in comparison group.	51% 77% (c)	49% 23% (c)	67% 78% (c)	33% 22% (c)
Positive values	Measures pro-social beliefs. Results = little improvement for both groups.	73% 80% (c)	27% 20% (c)	75% 80% (c)	25% 20% (c)
Social competencies	Measures perceived social skills. Results = little change in both groups.	85% 80% (c)	15% 20% (c)	80% 82% (c)	20% 18% (c)

Chapter Summary

Asset building really works. Risk can be markedly reduced and resiliency increased regardless of the challenges presented. The application of the Asset Checklist with powerful strategies and interventions in individual or group settings can produce powerful and tangible results.

References

American Academy of Child and Adolescent Psychiatry Council. (2010, June). *Principles of care for treatment of children and adolescents with mental illnesses in residential treatment centers.* Washington, DC: AACAP.

Coll, K.M., Sass, M., Freeman, B.J., Thobro, P., & Hauser, R. (2013). Treatment outcome differences between youth offenders from a rural Joint Commission accredited residential treatment center and a rural non-accredited center. *Residential Treatment for Children & Youth, 30*(3), 227–237.

Duke, N., Borowsky, I., Pettingell, S., & McMorris, B. (2011). Examining youth hopelessness as an independent risk correlate for adolescent delinquency and violence. *Maternal & Child Health Journal, 15*(1), 87–97.

Hawkins, J.D., Herrenkohl, T.I., Farrington, D.B., Brewer, F., Catalano, R.F., Harachi, T.W., & Cothern, L. (2000, April). Predictors of youth violence. *Juvenile Justice Bulletin,* 1–11.

Huizinga, D., Loeber, R., Thornberry, T.P., & Cothern, L. (2000, November). Co-occurrence of delinquency and other problem behaviors. *Juvenile Justice Bulletin,* 1–7.

McWhirter, J., McWhirter, B., McWhirter, E., & McWhirter, R. (2007). *At risk youth: A comprehensive response for counselors, teachers, psychologists, and human services professionals* (4th ed.). Belmont, CA: Thomson Brooks/Cole.

Search Institute. (2015). 40 developmental assets for adolescents. Retrieved December 6, 2016, from www.search-institute.org/content/40-developmental-assets-adolescents-ages-12-18.

Subramaniam, G.A., Lewis, L.L., Stitzer, M.L., & Fishman, M.J. (2004). Depressive symptoms in adolescents during residential treatment for substance abuse disorders. *The American Journal of Addictions, 13,* 256–267.

2

PSYCHOSOCIAL
DEVELOPMENT

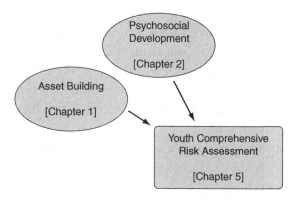

Key Learning Concepts
- Psychosocial development (key YCRA component)
- The MPD—measuring psychosocial development
- An early adolescence example
- A mid-adolescent example
- Best practice applications and an example of how to influence individual psychosocial development in a group setting

Mary and Ike: Developmentally Off-Track?

Mary is a guarded, lonely, physically mature 13-year-old, who is doing poorly in school and seemingly very sad. She wants very much to make friends, join the middle school band, and feel happier, yet her obstacles are challenging. She lives with her grandmother, sister, and dad, but reports that her dad is depressed and withdrawn from the family. She is argumentative with youth her age and with adults, she lacks confidence in her own ability to follow-through even on simple school projects, and she believes she has little to offer, especially to her younger sister, who is 10 years old. She is fiercely independent and likes to help others but she desperately needs to get, as she calls it, "traction before it's too late"; she is losing hope in herself.

Ike, at age 16, is a muscular, confident boy, good at making friends, and a natural leader. He wants to join the military, preferably as an officer. Yet his home and community environment are shaky at best. He lives with his dad in an area that is replete with crime, gang culture, and drug use, of which he has participated. His relationship with his mother, while close, is complicated by her legal problems. He very much needs to get a handle on his criminal behavior and drug use to have any hope of realizing his dreams.

Mary and Ike are real-life examples of youth struggling to make their way, to realize their goals, to thrive. They are not flourishing psychosocially.

Psychosocial Development

Psychosocial development is one of the three domains of development (along with biological and cognitive) and is defined as growing and positively adapting emotionally, in personality, with gender issues, and socially within the larger society (Berger, 1994).

An understanding of psychosocial development for adolescents is typically divided into three categories: early (ages 12–14), mid (ages 15–17), and late (ages 18–22). We are going to focus particularly on early and mid-adolescence here. Applying the psychosocial development lens is particularly important for helping professionals because this adolescent period is the most challenging and complicated period of life; in fact, psychosocial changes during the second decade of life show much greater diversity than biological and cognitive changes, as adolescents often struggle to develop their own identity, choosing from a vast number of sexual, moral, political, and educational paths (Berger, 1994). This second decade is so developmentally critical as the pivotal time of life because this is where the foundation of self-determination is formed.

Early Adolescence

Early adolescence begins at about age 12–13, lasting until about age 14 and is considered the most volatile stage of adolescence (Vernon, 1993). Characteristics of early adolescence typically include defensive, sensitive, and temperamental behaviors, often masking vulnerability and insecurity (Berger, 1994). Other psychosocial characteristics, as outlined by Vernon (1993), often include egocentricity, self-consciousness, and feelings of invincibility. Most notably, early adolescents begin to put peer relations in a dominant role and start the search for self (Berger, 1994).

Mid-Adolescence

Vernon (1993) noticed that in mid-adolescence, which corresponds to the high school years ages 15–17, the "yo-yo" nature of early adolescence is replaced by somewhat greater stability. Mid-adolescence is when teenagers try out adult roles. Thus major psychosocial tasks include acquiring a gender role, developing appropriate peer relations, developing emotional independence from parents, preparing for a career direction, and achieving socially responsible behavior. Poor previous psychosocial development often blankets a mid-adolescent's self-worth and makes successful accomplishment of such tasks difficult. Other psychosocial characteristics typically include experimentation (e.g., with drinking, smoking, sex), identity seeking (e.g., asking uniquely, who am I?), and striving for greater self-efficacy. Mid-adolescents also become aware of sexual feelings and become less egocentric (Vernon, 1993).

Relating to parents with new independence, to friends with new intimacy, and to oneself with new understanding are the key challenges for adolescents to attain adult status and maturity. Indeed, it is a deeply researched fact and a widely accepted operating principle in the helping professions that if too many and too difficult barriers to confident and smooth psychosocial development present themselves, that will negatively impact healthy psychosocial development (Hawley, 1988). The major conceptual model for understanding psychosocial development comes from the great psychologist Erik Erikson.

Erikson's Eight Developmental Processes

Erik Erikson's eight developmental processes are by far the most inclusive and frequently used constructs for understanding and studying psychosocial development. Presented in his first book (Erikson, 1963) and expanded in subsequent writings (Erikson, 1964, 1968, 1982), Erikson's theory continues to be the most valued, comprehensive account of psychosocial development. Based upon biographical and anthropological methods of study, Erikson's theory proposes that *every individual experiences eight developmental stages in the course of the life span*; they are listed in chronological order, referring to the developmental stages: trust vs. mistrust, autonomy vs. shame and doubt, initiative vs. guilt, industry vs. inferiority, identity vs. identity confusion, intimacy vs. isolation, generativity vs. stagnation, and ego integrity vs. despair. Each stage is marked by its own unique challenges, which is the result of interacting biological, psychological, and cultural forces. Reasons often cited for the widespread appeal and acceptance of Erikson's theory include its comprehensiveness, its specificity and predictability, its account for the complexity of personality development, its applicability to various academic and career fields, and its presentation of an optimistic view of personality (Coll, Thobro, & Haas, 2004).

Measuring Psychosocial Development

A terrific standardized assessment tool based on Eriksonian constructs that I have used with over 700 youth to date to assess psychosocial development is the Measure of Psychosocial Development (MPD), developed by Gwen Hawley (1988).

The MPD, a self-report inventory, provides an index of psychosocial health based on Erikson's criteria, and measures positive and negative developmental attitudes (Hawley, 1988). The MPD consists of 112 self-descriptive statements, can be completed in 15–20 minutes, and can be administered in individual or group formats (Hawley, 1988). Both reliability and validity for the MPD are robust (Hawley, 1988), that is to say, it is effective in measuring psychosocial development with youth in a variety of settings and from diverse backgrounds.

It is important to note that the MPD assesses developmental stages for adolescents typically associated with later life according to Erikson's model (e.g., generativity vs. stagnation, ego integrity vs. despair). This approach is based on Erikson's theoretical notion, verified by Hawley (1988), that *youth need a reasonable disposition toward later stages* to develop in a psychosocially healthy manner.

Mary (Early Adolescent Example)

Let's now apply these psychosocial concepts and the MPD by listening in on a therapeutic conversation with Mary, the 13-year-old introduced at the beginning of the chapter. Mary fits many of the described early adolescent challenges, such as defensiveness, sensitivity, temperamental behaviors, and accenting peer relations. First, here is a brief description of Mary's MPD results.

Mary's MPD Results

Mary has scored herself very low in certain key developmental stages—trust vs. mistrust, industry vs. inferiority, intimacy vs. isolation, generativity vs. stagnation, and ego integrity vs. despair (all below the 10th percentile, where the 50th percentile is considered average). She also reports carrying around a lot of negative emotions—mistrust, inferiority, stagnation, despair—which are all above the 90th percentile as compared to youth her age (50th considered average). Mary does bring psychosocial developmental strengths to the table as well, including

solid resolution of autonomy vs. shame and doubt, and strong
generativity, meaning she has a very solid willingness and desire
to help others. Let's see if we can get a glimpse of how we can
use this psychosocial developmental conceptualization to identify
doorways to help Mary. Note, I will provide commentary/identify
developmental weaknesses within the dialogue.

CO = Counselor

M = Mary

CO: I am curious about something ... you got a bit emotional
        when you were talking to your grandmother about
        your dad.

M: Yeah I did.

CO: What role would you like him to play in your life?

M: Honestly I don't care anymore. (*lack of trust*)

CO: Don't care ... what do you mean?

M: I mean he can be part of my life but I don't know exactly
        what role he would fit into. (*an autonomous view*)

CO: You said that when you were 10 you felt like you did things
        together ... fishing, other things.

M: Sort of after a couple of years we just stopped doing things
        together and ... I don't know.

CO: It's interesting 'cause it's about the same time you started
        to struggle with motivation, going to school, right? (*lack
        of initiative, industry*)

M: Umm it's around that time, yeah about the same time.

CO: Do you think it is related?

M: No. I don't know if it had earlier effects, maybe it did, I
        couldn't tell you.

CO: What was it like for you when he just stopped ... ?

M: Umm, I guess I didn't really notice, 'cause I started doing
        more things with friends, like I was growing up. So I was
        hanging out more with friends more than when I was
        younger and home all the time, so I guess I didn't
        notice. (*working on intimacy development*)

CO: Didn't notice?

M:· Yeah, I was always asking but he was always saying we'll do it at a later time or something. (*a blow to intimacy development*)

CO: So you were asking to do things with him and he kept putting you off. Was it the same way with your sister too?

M: Yeah, we always wanted to do things with him like go hiking or fishing.

CO: Was he, you shared with me before that he drinks a lot, was he drinking at this point?

M: Umm yeah I think he was. I mean he has been drinking since I can remember, I'd say I think when him and my mom got divorced he started drinking more. I just grew up with my dad so I got used to it. (*barrier to supporting Mary's overall development*)

Interventions

We become aware that the withdrawal of her father's attention and his drinking has probably greatly disrupted Mary's psychosocial development, especially related to intimacy and industry development. How can we help her get back on track in these areas while supporting her developmental strengths in autonomy and generativity?

Through a review of best practices in the professional literature (Jongsma, Peterson, & McInnis, 2003) we strategized the following individualized plan for Mary. Over a period of eight weeks, the helping professional working with Mary instituted the following:

- acted as a parent surrogate, not as a buddy
- expressed respect, interest, concern for Mary's point of view
- helped Mary identify and express her negative feelings and emotions.

Let's listen to the progress being made with the application of these interventions (here at the fifth week).

M: I guess I am confused on how to feel. I guess all the sadness is all coming up from back then. (*dealing with negative emotions of stagnation, inferiority, despair*)

CO: Okay so the sadness you are experiencing now is coming from back when you were 10 and you felt like you lost your dad to drinking…

M: 'Cause even back then I kept it in, I never really talked about it, ever.

CO: Sounds like it was pretty painful.

M: Yeah … it was.

CO: What did you do with that sadness?

M: I just pushed it away … passed it off.

CO: I see it coming out now.

M: I guess this is the first time I ever really thought about it and let it out.

CO: How does it feel to talk about it? Is it okay?

M: Yeah it's okay.

CO: Do you feel like it may be helpful?

M: Yeah.

CO: If dad was on the phone, what do you want to say to him?

M: Stop drinking.

CO: Stop drinking … Because?

M: I want to spend time with you.

CO: I want to spend time with you … because?

M: I love you. (*promoting intimacy development through expression of emotions*)

CO: I love you and?

M: Umm I miss him.

CO: You miss him?

M: Yeah…

CO: You never did that, you never told him…

M: No.

CO: You just held it in like most 10-year-olds probably would.

M: Yeah.

In talking with Mary a few months after the end of counseling, she expressed being able to unload these emotions, especially sadness, and breaking through in her understanding that these feelings are OK, are normal, don't have to control her, and can be managed. This is a good example of Mary starting the important search for self (Berger, 1994). Although she still struggles with making friends, and her dad continues to struggle with his drinking and depression, Mary is noticeably better groomed, now has joined the school band, and is better able to use her developmental strength of autonomy and generativity to volunteer at a local nursing home, which has had the fortunate consequence of increasing her industry. Mary is well on her way to a healthier psychosocial developmental path.

Ike (Mid-Adolescent Example)

Ike is a confident 16-year-old, but according to his MPD results, he may be masking some psychosocial struggles. First, a brief description of the results of Ike's MPD; then, we'll listen in.

Ike's MPD Results

Ike sees himself as pretty good in resolving most developmental stages—except industry vs. inferiority, generativity vs. stagnation (below the 10th percentile, again where the 50th is considered average). He too is carrying around some strong negative emotions, especially mistrust, shame and doubt, identity confusion, stagnation, and despair, all above the 90th percentile as compared to his peers (50th is average). Ike's psychosocial strengths are his strong resolution of initiative vs. guilt and intimacy vs. isolation, meaning that he will initiate action for himself and others and that he values and is confident about making and maintaining close interpersonal relationships. Let's see if we can get a sense of Ike in this context and how to help him, especially with identity development.

CO: How was it, seeing friends?

I: Um, it was pretty cool. I mean, I didn't talk to any, like, friend friends. You know?

CO: What are "friend friends"?

I: Like, smoke weed … "Bad friends—just get high friends." I just talked to some friends. (*identity confusion*)

CO: So what are these friends versus pot smoking friends?

I: They're just, actual friends. I talked to my mom on the phone, too. (*intimacy*)

CO: Oh. That's pretty major. That's the first time in a while?

I: Yeah. I told her, well, she messaged me on Facebook. I was like, just call me. And I gave her my number. And I talked to her. I told her about everything. So, it was pretty cool.

CO: So what came of that conversation? Tell me about it.

I: Um, it was, it was pretty good. We just like, talked about how she's doing, how I'm doing, we just kind of BS'd for a little bit.

CO: What kind of things did you share with her? About how you're doing?

I: Um, I told her how much improvement I've made. Uh, I'm a lot different than I was six months ago. Stuff like that. Little things. My mom told me she got a job. She's doing good, nobody knows if there's a warrant out for her anymore. (*despair*)

CO: Is this still a worry? The warrant stuff?

I: Yeah, kind of. I don't know. (*shame and doubt*)

Interventions

We also notice that Ike has friends ("good and bad") and seems socially very adept. But we also become aware that there is a pull for Ike toward his ("bad") weed-smoking friends and he feels deep shame and doubt, worry and despair about his mom's legal troubles even as he was glad to connect with her. How can we help him with his negative emotions and identity while supporting his strong development in initiative and intimacy?

We developed Ike's plan with the following best practices:

- encouraging examination of each (family) relationship related to developing empathy for the other person's

perceptions, encouraging consideration of how current
perceptions and expectations arise from childhood
experiences and the internalized messages from others,
and helping in recognizing that the negative self-images
are derived from past painful experience and can be
changed (Bowlby, 1988).
- helping increase inner-directedness (Jongsma et al.,
  2003).

Let's listen to the progress being made with Ike.

CO: Your mom's legal trouble, is it your worry? Or a shared
       worry (with her)?
I: I think there is with my mom too; I didn't know till she told
       me that she feels really guilty and sad about what she
       has put me through. My mom is going to work and stuff
       now, so they (legal authorities) are working with her.
CO: She sounds...?
I: Good.
CO: How does it feel to talk to her more and more?
I: I feel really good. I want her to be happy.
CO: So what happened to the anxiety and worry you've been
       having?
I: It just went away. I don't know. I told her when I'm going to
       visit her next month. I think we'll visit more then.
CO: So some of that worry went away, you are having good
       conversations with her, and you set up a face-to-face
       visit. (*initiative*) Once you connect with her, what hap-
       pens to that anxiety?
I: It just goes away.
CO: It just goes away? Kind of like a switch? Like an on/off
       switch?
I: Yeah.

This is a good example of Ike reducing his shame and doubt by
taking his mom's perspective and allowing her to take his. This

exchange also illustrates that he is growing "inner-directedness" by examining his feelings and acting positively on them, by engaging his mom, rather than blaming himself and her. Over the next few months, Ike maintained his strong initiative and intimacy development while increasing his industry (better school performance). His mom continues to not violate parole and is holding a job. While he does not live with her, Ike talks with her every day on the phone and visits her at least once a month. He has not re-offended and is making plans for Reserve Officer Training Corps (ROTC).

Helping Individual Development in Group Settings

We recently used the MPD as a pre-test and post-test measure to conduct a study at an alternative middle and high school for youth struggling with school drop-out. We tested the youth when they first entered the school, then staff consistently used the following best practices for each developmental area as illustrated below using a *checklist* weekly to maintain consistency and re-tested them after six months. We tracked early adolescents (middle school youth) separately from mid-adolescents (high school youth).

Best Practice Applications

TRUST VS. MISTRUST

Helpful interactions to *increase trust and reduce mistrust* (Hawkins, Catalano, & Miller, 1992; Ranieri, 1984) are as follows:

- Act as a parent surrogate not as a buddy.
- Set firm limits for acceptable behavior.
- Help in practical matters, such as schoolwork, employment, and particularly socialization.
- Acknowledge similar problems you have encountered.
- Encourage youth involvement in active classroom instruction.
- Emphasize interactive teaching and cooperative learning.
- Use tutoring of the socially rejected youth.

- Build social competency skills with adolescents in need.
- Provide peer resistance training.

INITIATIVE VS. GUILT/INDUSTRY VS. INFERIORITY

- Identify positive behaviors (don't use discouragers); focusing on the specific deed.
- Use the language of encouragement.
- Focus on what the adolescent is good at and interested in.
- Then create pro-social ways to help him or her express them by using a sound career guidance process (Carlson & Lewis, 1994; Center for Substance Abuse Treatment, 1997).

GENERATIVITY VS. STAGNATION

John Bowlby's (1988) therapeutic tasks for building better attachment:

- Provide the client with a secure base (a safe and trusting environment) to explore the various unhappy and painful life aspects.
- Encourage positive ways to engage in relationships with loved ones.

EGO INTEGRITY VS. DESPAIR

- Assess level of depression (Coll et al., 2004).
- Explore secondary gains (i.e., what is the positive side of this?) (Miller & Rollnick, 2002).
- Check for depression within the first month in those who present low ego integrity scores (below 15% and high despair scores, above 86%); note: depressed adolescents show very different symptomology than adults, with fewer verbal expressions of depression, and with disruptive behaviors (Capuzzi & Gross, 1996).
- Focus on increasing sense of self-worth and reducing isolation.

- Teach stress management.
- Encourage better communication and problem-solving skills.
- Encourage development of religious faith and church participation if interest is there (Butler, 1997).
- Find genuine reasons to like, respect, and admire the adolescent.
- Use genuine empathic responses and affirmations (Miller, 1994; Miller & Rollnick, 2002).

Psychosocial Developmental Differences at School Admission between Early and Mid-Adolescents

Consistent with the literature (Vernon, 1993), early adolescents indicated *significantly more* psychosocial distress than mid-adolescents. Specific areas of significantly more distress (and less development) were in the areas of trust vs. mistrust, identity vs. identity confusion, intimacy vs. isolation, generativity vs. stagnation, and ego integrity vs. despair. There were no significant differences at admission between early and mid-adolescents in autonomy vs. shame and doubt, initiative vs. guilt, and industry vs. inferiority.

Psychosocial Developmental Changes after Six Months (Early and Mid-Adolescents)

EARLY ADOLESCENTS

Early adolescents indicated significant statistical change over six months in total psychosocial development, and in the specific developmental areas of trust vs. mistrust, initiative vs. guilt, identity vs. identity confusion, and ego integrity vs. despair (at least a 20% improvement in these areas). No significant gains after six months of treatment were made in the areas of autonomy vs. shame and doubt, industry vs. inferiority, intimacy vs. isolation, and generativity vs. stagnation.

MID-ADOLESCENTS

Mid-adolescents also indicated significant change after six months of treatment in total psychosocial development, as well as in *all of the specific developmental* areas (at least a 20% jump in all areas).

Clearly, active use of psychosocial developmental best practices in school settings has a big payoff, especially for mid-adolescents. Early adolescents are more of a challenge and did not make the kind of progress we hoped for. However, the half-full glass is the four areas where progress was made. Undoubtedly, more staff training about working with this challenging time of ages 12–14 is warranted and specific strategies to improve areas of autonomy vs. shame and doubt, industry vs. inferiority, intimacy vs. isolation, and generativity vs. stagnation for early adolescents are especially needed.

Chapter Summary

The key learning concepts of psychosocial development were presented, including Erik Erikson's eight developmental stages, steps for measuring psychosocial development, and applications with early and mid-adolescent examples. A best practice application and an example of how to influence individual psychosocial development in a school setting were also included.

References

Berger, K.S. (1994). *The developing person through the life span* (3rd ed.). New York, NY: Worth.

Bowlby, J. (1988). *A secure base.* London: Basic Books.

Butler, K. (1997, March/April). The anatomy of resilience. *Networker*, 22–31.

Capuzzi, D., & Gross, D.R. (1996). *Youth at risk* (2nd ed.). Alexandria, VA: ACA.

Carlson, J., & Lewis, J. (1994). *Counseling the adolescent.* Denver, CO: Love.

Center for Substance Abuse Treatment. (1997). *50 strategies for substance abuse treatment.* Rockville, MD: USDHHS.

Coll, K.M., Thobro, P., & Haas, R. (2004). Relational and purpose development in youth offenders. *Journal of Humanistic Counseling, Education and Development, 43*, 41–49.

Erikson, E. (1963). *Childhood and society* (2nd ed.). New York, NY: Norton.

Erikson, E. (1964). *Insight and responsibility.* New York, NY: Norton.

Erikson, E. (1968). *Identity: Youth and crisis.* New York, NY: Norton.

Erikson, E. (1982). *The life cycle completed.* New York, NY: Norton.

Hawkins, J.D., Catalano, R.F., & Miller, J.Y. (1992) Risk and protective factors for alcohol and other drug problems in adolescence and early adulthood: Implications for substance abuse prevention. *Psychological Bulletin, 112,* 54–105.

Hawley, G. (1988). *Measures of Psychosocial Development manual.* Lutz, FL: Psychological Assessment Resources.

Jongsma, A., Peterson, L., & McInnis, W. (2003). *The adolescent psychotherapy treatment planner* (3rd ed.). Hoboken, NJ: John Wiley & Sons, Inc.

Miller, F. (1994). *Substance Abuse Subtle Screening Inventory (SASSI) manual.* Bloomington, IN: SASSI Institute.

Miller, W.R., & Rollnick, S. (2002). *Motivational interviewing: Preparing people for change* (2nd ed.). New York, NY: Guilford Press.

Ranieri, R. (1984). Motivating institutionalized adolescents for psychotherapy. *Adolescence, 19,* 925–933.

Vernon, A. (1993). *Development assessment and intervention with children and adolescents.* Alexandria, VA: ACA.

3

FAMILY ENGAGEMENT

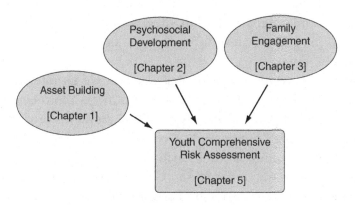

> **Key Learning Concepts**
> - Family as a system
> - Engagement vs. conflict
> - Assessment—The FACES III (key YCRA component)
> - The Murray family
> - Applying FACES III and WDEP concepts

Family as a Dynamic System

It is no coincidence that improving family relationships played a key role in helping the youth discussed in the previous two chapters. The facts are that adolescents are participating members in a larger dynamic family system, and emotional experiences are interdependent and influenced by family interactions (Gunderson & Lyons-Ruth, 2008). In other words, a child's world at the individual level is also comprised of a shared world at the family level. Over time, emotions and behavior of any one family member are the result of a *three-way interaction* between 1) his or her own emotional processes, 2) those of the persons he or she is interacting with, and 3) the emotional character of the interaction itself (Chassin & Handley, 2006). For example, if 1) a youth comes home from school feeling rejected and sad because of bullying at school and tells his dad about it, then 2) his dad responds by saying "That's dumb, don't feel that way," the youth will likely 3) feel rejection and sadness more intensely (result of emotional character of the interaction) and may respond by saying "no, you're dumb," and conflict emerges.

Struggling youth in particular may be vulnerable to poor family engagement, defined as low emotional connectedness and attunement among members. Often conflict is present in a struggling youth's family and of course has negative effects on family engagement and individual development per this described three-way interaction (Coll, Thobro, & Haas, 2004). If family conflict is chronic and parents respond to the youth's challenging behaviors with harsh, negative, and inconsistent parenting styles, then aversive and aggressive behavior on the part of the youth becomes likely, and as in the example, hostile interaction often leads to further poor family engagement and emotional connectedness (McWhirter, McWhirter, McWhirter, & McWhirter, 2007).

Engagement, Cohesion, and Conflict

Healthy family engagement is exhibited by parent–child communication that is open and relaxed, particularly about experiences of positive and negative emotions (Kerns, Tomich, Aspelmeier, & Contreras, 2000). Family cohesion is described in terms of family members' capacities to emotionally respond to each other in ways that are accurate and developmentally meaningful. In other words, healthy families share a "state of mind" that enables them to maintain a balance between shared emotional connection on the one hand and individuality on the other (Cobner & Hill, 2003). Back to the previous three-way interaction, if Dad's response (the second part) was something like "Wow, that's very hurtful, tell me more," engagement and cohesion are strengthened (part 3), and potential for conflict is greatly reduced. Secure family engagement and cohesion enable youth to acknowledge distress, engage in constructive problem-solving behavior, seek support from others, and regulate emotions (Richmond & Stocker, 2006; Buist, Dekovic, Meeus, & Van Aken, 2004).

Large-scale studies have discovered that peer relational learning in adolescence is highly influenced by the level of family engagement and perceived emotional availability of family members (Coll, Juhnke, Thobro, Haas, & Smith-Robinson, 2008; Trumpeter, Watson, O'Leary, & Weathington, 2008). It should be noted that adolescents' *perceptions* of engagement and cohesion, rather than overt parental behaviors or intentions, are found to have the greatest impact on the development of trust and intimacy (Trumpeter et al., 2008). However, we also know that certain parental behavior responses, such as attentiveness, listening, displaying patience, and speaking calmly, contribute greatly to positive perceptions on the youth's part.

Long-term consequences of family conflict have been well documented. Indeed, longitudinal studies reveal that adolescents whose families were marked with conflict are more likely to develop severe externalizing behaviors (i.e., delinquency and aggression) compared to adolescents from more cohesive families. They are also more likely to drop out of school and face adversity across multiple domains of functioning, including mental health, interpersonal relationships, family functioning, and socioeconomic status, and additionally, without appropriate intervention, these conditions are likely to continue into adulthood (Colman, Kim, Mitchell-Herzfeld, & Shady, 2009). For example, there is strong evidence that family conflict creates disruptions in the formation of emotional regulation and has been linked to a number of adolescent psychosocial issues, including depression and suicide (Steinberg & Davila, 2008;

Taliaferro, Rienzo, Pigg, Miller, & Dodd, 2009), conduct dis-order (Chen & Simons-Morton, 2009; Coll et al., 2008), self-injurious behavior (Crowell et al., 2008), and substance use disorders (Coll et al., 2004; Tucker, Ellickson, & Klein, 2008). Needless to say, when trying to help struggling youth, it is important to assess levels of perceived cohesion and engagement.

Assessment

The Family Adaptability and Cohesion Evaluation Scales-III

The Family Adaptability and Cohesion Evaluation Scales-III (FACES III) is a very effective and simple tool that is often used to measure the level of family functioning as perceived by family members (Maynard & Olson, 1987). The FACES III is a self-report questionnaire that consists of 20 items (with a Likert-type scale ranging from 1 to 4) developed for use with adolescents as young as 12 years of age. The FACES III has demonstrated strong test-retest reliability (0.83) and discriminate validity (Olson, 1986). The FACES III consists of two scales: the Adapta-bility Scale and the Cohesion Scale.

The Cohesion Scale is the focus here and consists of 10 items. The Cohesion Scale score is used to determine levels of family engagement and cohesion (i.e., the level of family connected-ness and emotional bonding). The Cohesion Scale ranges from extremely low, disengaged (10–31) to more moderate levels, separated (32–37) and connected (38–43) to extremely high, enmeshed (44–50). Examples of items include: "Family mem-bers like to spend free time with each other," "Family members ask each other for help," and "Family members feel closer to other family members than people outside the family."

Meet the "Murray" Family

The Murrays (not their real name) are in trouble. Family coun-seling has been court-mandated because Roberta has been arrested for minor-in-possession violations and truancy. Mom is struggling as a single parent since her divorce two years ago. Mom, sister (Roberta), age 16, brother (Karl), age 14, and two more little children (ages 7 and 5) make up the family unit. Roberta is currently not going to school and is involved in substance abuse and delinquent behavior. Karl is cutting himself and exhibiting signs of depression. Each has differing views of engagement and cohesion, and conflict abounds. Results of the FACES III show Roberta and Karl scoring "disengaged," with scores of 22 and 24 respectively, and Mom scoring 33, "separated." Let's listen in on a very effective intervention using the FACES III and an approach by William Glasser (2000), called WDEP (Wants, Doing, Evaluating, Plan). Note, the counselor will explain this in the dialogue below.

C = Counselor
M = Mom
R = Roberta
K = Karl

C: Mom, I think you're saying you feel upset by how the children seem to move to conflict very quickly—especially Roberta and Karl. They yell at each other and the little ones, and when this happens, your tendency is to withdrawal, often into your room till things die down.

M: Yeah, that's it. It's embarrassing I guess. I'm really tired when I get home. I do want to connect with my kids, but when they go at each other, I just want to run away.

C: That's understandable, you're tired and don't want to deal with all of this fighting. On the other hand, I notice Roberta and Karl are saying through the assessment all of you took last week (FACES III) that they want more closeness as a family. Yet with all this yelling and conflict, it's hard to figure out how to get there…

C: It may be helpful to first diagram an example of a three-way interaction I see between you, Mom, and each of you, Roberta and Karl. Let's start with you, Roberta: 1) Mom comes home and you are upset and want to tell her that Missy, the five-year-old, is not working on the list you left for her and is always saying "you're not the boss of me" ..., 2) Mom, you're feeling particularly exhausted and had a tough day and say, "Oh just let it go tonight, Roberta," then 3) Roberta, you feel angry and say "Fine! But don't ask me to continue to babysit her all the time." Mom, you're feeling put-upon and, Roberta, you're feeling angry and not appreciated. Is that accurate? And if so, what behavior does this dynamic tend to create in you? Roberta, you go first.

R: Yes, it makes me so angry. Mom, I don't know what to do with Missy. I guess when this happens, I usually go and tell Missy that I'm not going to deal with her s..., Karl then tells me to quit being ridiculous, I go for him then.

M: This is accurate for me, Roberta seems so angry all the time, I just go into my room and run a bath so I can't hear all the yelling.

C: OK, we'll talk about how to break this pattern, but let's do an illustration with Karl, are you ready? 1) Mom comes home and you're feeling excited because you got a really good grade in math and want to tell her, 2) Mom, you're again feeling exhausted and say, "That's nice, Karl, can you calm your sister (Roberta) down?," then 3) Karl, you feel rejected and say "OK, I guess...". Mom, you're feeling overwhelmed and, Karl, you're feeling not just rejected but sad too. Is that accurate? And if so, what behavior does this dynamic tend to create in you? Karl, you go first.

K: Yes, I can't control Roberta anyway. I usually try to help but it doesn't work.

M: I didn't know this was happening. I just am so tired sometimes I don't have the energy I guess.

K: Mom, I know you're tired but I need more leadership from you on this.

R: Yeah mom, when we're yelling I need you to go over and do something because I don't know what to do...

M: I hear that, but when I'm just about ready to open my mouth sometimes I don't do it because I don't want to lose my temper and I'm not sure how I'm going to do it. It's easier to go take a bath…

C: Yeah maybe in the heat of the moment there's a calm suggestion you could come up with that makes sense, but it's hard to think of it.

C: I really appreciate this honest and frank discussion. It is clear to me you all care deeply about each other and making change for the better is very important. I want to introduce a little structure this week that I think will reduce conflict and increase consistency and also what you all want—more *family bonding*.

C: To break these negative three-way interactions we just talked about, and to increase family engagement per the items you each endorsed on the FACES III, I want to introduce another concept called WDEP (Wants, Doing, Evaluating, Plan). The best way I can think of to explain the WDEP is to walk though this following table (counselor explained the WDEP table, shown in Table 3.1 below).

C: Now that we have the "What do I want, how am I going about trying to get that, and is [what I'm doing] working," the WDE part of WDEP, let's really concentrate on the P—Plan to implement this week.

M: This is the structure we need, I think?

C: Very good, let's start with something very do-able, like structuring how, when, and what it will look like to spend some free time together this week as a family.

C: Mom, I know you probably don't get much free time and I know that's a challenge.

M: I have Sundays.

C: Could you, Mom, spend a little free time on Sunday with Karl and spend a little free time with Roberta? Would that be a more effective way for you to better meet your wants—feeling closer, and less conflict?

Table 3.1 **Wants, Doing, Evaluating, Plan (WDEP)**

	Mom	*Roberta*	*Karl*
What do I want (per the FACES III)? (W)	Feeling closer, less conflict	More time doing something fun together, feeling closer	More time doing something fun together, feeling closer
What am I doing to get what I want? (D)	Walking away, going to my room and taking a bath	Acting up to get Mom's attention	Arguing with sister, withdrawing, hoping Mom will notice
Is what I am currently doing working? (E)valuating	No	No	No
What can I do that could be better at getting my "wants" met? NEW (P)lan			

M: Yes, I definitely want some time alone with Karl and some time alone with Roberta.

C: Are you two OK with that? Does that address your wants?

R: Yeah, like when I'm alone with Mom I could be talking about my stuff...

K: Me too, sounds great.

C: How much alone time do you want?

K: 20–45 minutes maybe.

R: Yeah.

C: 20–45 minutes and you're willing to really talk with your mom during the designated time? Saying, "I don't want to talk right now" would be bad, you know what I mean? Is that OK?

R and K: Yes.

C: What about family time? Can you do that as well on Sunday?

M: I'd really like that we talked about working on a family dinner together before but just never set it up.

C: It doesn't happen unless you have some kind of structure and plan—here's the opportunity. So Sundays are alone time and joint, family time.

C: One meal on Sunday. Which one?

M: Dinner, I think.

R: Uh-huh (yes).

C: OK then the goal. Now let's look at the assignments.

M: For that meal we have to include to clean up afterwards.

C: Yeah, let me write all of this down.

Table 3.2 **WDEP: Plan**

	Mom	*Roberta*	*Karl*
What can I do that could be better at getting my "wants" met? NEW (P)lan	Sunday—20–45 minutes each with R and K; family dinner with assignments for all the kids.	20–45 minutes of alone time with Mom—talk about stuff on my mind; cooperatively do my bit for the family dinner with a no conflict rule.	20–45 minutes of alone time with Mom—talk about stuff on my mind; cooperatively do my bit for the family dinner with a no conflict rule.

M: Yeah, I feel really good about this. Thanks, Roberta and Karl.

C: Alright! Remember this is an experiment and we'll all learn some things from it. When we talk next week we can analyze how it went per the WDEP model and we can adjust if needed. Great work, everyone!

Chapter Summary

Given the complexities of family dynamics, it is imperative for counselors to use a great deal of concreteness. For the helping professional, keep an "eye on the ball," in this case, breaking the negative three-way interactions, promoting all getting their "wants" met appropriately, and noting evidence of increased family cohesion and reduced conflict. By the way, the Murray family was much happier three months down the road and doing much better (all significantly improved on their FACES III cohesion scores)—they just needed greater awareness, a good plan, and follow-through.

References

Buist, K.L., Dekovic, M., Meeus, W.H., & Van Aken, M.A. (2004). Attachment in adolescence: A social relations model analysis. *Journal of Adolescent Research, 19*(6), 826–850.

Chassin, L., & Handley, E.D. (2006). Parents and families as contexts for the development of substance use and substance use disorders. *Psychology of Addictive Behaviors, 20*(2), 135–137.

Chen, R., & Simons-Morton, B. (2009). Concurrent changes in conduct problems and depressive symptoms in early adolescents: A developmental person-centered approach. *Development and Psychopathology, 21*(1), 285–307.

Cobner, R., & Hill, J. (2003). Review of what works for whom? A critical review of treatments for children and adolescents. *Clinical Child Psychology and Psychiatry, 8*(4), 557–559.

Coll, K.M., Juhnke, G.A., Thobro, P., Haas, R., & Smith-Robinson (2008). Family disengagement of youth offenders: Implications for counselors. *The Family Journal, 16*(4), 359–363.

Coll, K.M., Thobro, P., & Haas, R. (2004). Relational and purpose development in youth offenders. *Journal of Humanistic Counseling, Education, and Development, 43*, 41–49.

Colman, R., Kim, D.H., Mitchell-Herzfeld, S., & Shady, T.A. (2009). Delinquent girls grown up: Young adult offending patterns and their relation to early legal, individual, and family risk. *Journal of Youth and Adolescence, 38*(3), 355–366.

Crowell, S.E., Beauchaine, T.P., McCauley, E., Smith, C.J., Vasilev, C.A., & Stevens, A.L. (2008). Parent-child interactions, peripheral serotonin, and self-inflicted injury in adolescents. *Journal of Consulting and Clinical Psychology, 76*(1), 15–21.

Glasser, W. (2000). *Reality therapy in action*. New York, NY: HarperCollins Publishers.

Gunderson J.G., & Lyons-Ruth, K. (2008). BPD's interpersonal hypersensitivity phenotype: A gene-environment-developmental model. *Journal of Personality Disorders, 22*(1), 22–41.

Kerns, K.A., Tomich, P.L., Aspelmeier, J.E., & Contreras, J.M. (2000). Attachment based assessments of parent-child relationships in middle childhood. *Developmental Psychology, 36*(5), 614–626.

Maynard, P.E., & Olson, D.H. (1987). Circumplex model of family systems: A treatment tool in family counseling. *Journal of Counseling and Development, 65*(9), 502–504.

McWhirter, J., McWhirter, B., McWhirter, E., & McWhirter, R. (2007). *At risk youth: A comprehensive response for counselors, teachers, psychologists, and human services professionals* (4th ed.). Belmont, CA: Thomson Brooks/Cole.

Olson, D.H. (1986). Circumplex model VII: Validation studies and FACES III. *Family Process, 25*(3), 337–351.

Richmond, M.K., & Stocker, C.M. (2006). Associations between family cohesion and adolescent siblings' externalizing behavior. *Journal of Family Psychology, 20*(4), 663–669.

Steinberg, S.J., & Davila, J. (2008). Romantic functioning and depressive symptoms among early adolescent girls: The moderating role of parental emotional availability. *Journal of Clinical Child and Adolescent Psychology, 37*(2), 350–362.

Taliaferro, L.A., Rienzo, B.A., Pigg, R.M. Miller, M.D., & Dodd, V.J. (2009). Associations between physical activity and reduced rates of hopelessness, depression, and suicidal behavior among college students. *Journal of the American College Health Association, 57*(4), 427–435.

Trumpeter, N.N., Watson, P.J., O'Leary, B.J., & Weathington, B.L. (2008). Self-functioning and perceived parenting: Relations of parental empathy and love inconsistency with narcissism, depression, and self-esteem. *The Journal of Genetic Psychology: Research and Theory on Human Development, 169*(1), 51–71.

Tucker, J., Ellickson, P.L., & Klein, D.J. (2008). Growing up in a permissive household: What deters at-risk adolescents from heavy drinking. *Journal of Studies on Alcohol and Drugs, 69*(4), 528–534.

4

COMMON BEHAVIORAL
ISSUES AND THEIR
MANIFESTATIONS

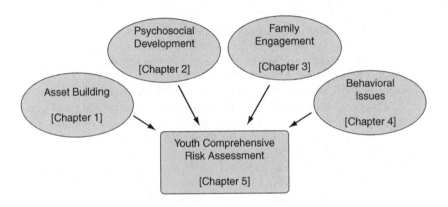

Key Learning Concepts
- Conduct disordered behavior and criminal thinking (key YCRA components)
  - Assessment tools
- Substance abuse (key YCRA component)
  - Assessment tool
- Trauma (key YCRA component)
  - Assessment tool
- A case study—Assessment in action and applying interventions to reduce problem behaviors and increase positive behaviors: motivational enhancement and trauma focused strategies

When youth are referred for help, often they are identified because of behavioral problems, and many are in legal trouble. Common behavioral problems revolve around substance abuse, and what are called conduct disordered behaviors and their accompanying attitude issues. The context and extent of these problems are important to systematically identify. It is also important for helping professionals to delve below the surface to gauge how much traumatic distress is driving the problematic behaviors and attitudes. I have found three very accessible and useful assessments to accomplish this task.

Conduct Disordered Behavior and Assessment

Behaviors symptomatic of *conduct disorder* can be easily assessed by qualified professionals using previous records and by creating a DSM-V (APA, 2013) conduct disordered checklist (see below). A brief interview can be then be conducted with the youth. Such an assessment using the DSM-V criteria has been recommended in the literature as an effective way for assessment and monitoring conduct disorder behaviors (Miller, Trapani, Fejes-Mendoza, Eggleston, & Dwiggins, 1995; Zoccolillo & Rogers, 1991).

Table 4.1 DSM-V™ diagnostic criteria

Conduct disorder

1   A repetitive and persistent pattern of behavior in which the basic rights of others or major age-appropriate societal norms or rules are violated, as manifested by the presence of at least three of the following 15 criteria in the past 12 months from any of the categories below, with at least one criterion present in the past six months:

Aggression to people and animals
   1   Often bullies, threatens, or intimidates others.
   2   Often initiates physical fights.
   3   Has used a weapon that can cause serious physical harm to others (e.g., a bat, brick, broken bottle, knife, gun).
   4   Has been physically cruel to people.
   5   Has been physically cruel to animals.
   6   Has stolen while confronting a victim (e.g., mugging, purse snatching, extortion, armed robbery).
   7   Has forced someone into sexual activity.

Destruction of property
   8   Has deliberately engaged in fire setting with the intention of causing serious damage.

Table 4.1 **Continued**

Conduct disorder

9   Has deliberately destroyed others' property (other than by fire setting).

Deceitfulness or theft
10   Has broken into someone else's house, building, or car.
11   Often lies to obtain goods or favors or to avoid obligations (i.e., "cons" others).
12   Has stolen items of nontrivial value without confronting a victim (e.g., shoplifting, but without breaking and entering; forgery).

Serious violations of rules
13   Often stays out at night despite parental prohibitions, beginning before age 13 years.
14   Has run away from home overnight at least twice while living in the parental or parental surrogate home, or once without returning for a lengthy period.
15   Is often truant from school, beginning before age 13 years.

2   The disturbance in behavior causes clinically significant impairment in social, academic, or occupational functioning.
3   If the individual is age 18 years or older, criteria are not met for antisocial personality disorder.

Specify whether:
312.81 (F91.1) Childhood-onset type: Individuals show at least one symptom characteristic of conduct disorder prior to age 10 years.

312.82 (F91.2) Adolescent-onset type: Individuals show no symptom characteristic of conduct disorder prior to age 10 years.

312.89 (F91.9) Unspecified onset: Criteria for a diagnosis of conduct disorder are met, but there is not enough information available to determine whether the onset of the first symptom was before or after age 10 years.

Specify if:
With limited pro-social emotions: To qualify for this specifier, an individual must have displayed at least two of the following characteristics persistently over at least 12 months and in multiple relationships and settings. These characteristics reflect the individual's typical pattern of interpersonal and emotional functioning over this period and not just occasional occurrences in some situations. Thus, to assess the criteria for the specifier, multiple information sources are necessary. In addition to the individual's self-report, it is necessary to consider reports by others who have known the individual for extended periods of time (e.g., parents, teachers, co-workers, extended family members, peers).

Lack of remorse or guilt: Does not feel bad or guilty when he or she does something wrong (exclude remorse when expressed only when caught and/or facing punishment). The individual shows a general lack of concern about the negative consequences of his or her actions. For example, the individual is not remorseful after hurting someone or does not care about the consequences of breaking rules.

Callous—lack of empathy: Disregards and is unconcerned about the feelings of others. The individual is described as cold and uncaring. The person appears more concerned about the effects of his or her actions on himself or herself, rather than their effects on others, even when they result in substantial harm to others.

Unconcerned about performance: Does not show concern about poor/problematic performance at school, at work, or in other important activities. The individual does not put forth the effort necessary to perform well, even when expectations are clear, and typically blames others for his or her poor performance.

Shallow or deficient affect: Does not express feelings or show emotions to others, except in ways that seem shallow, insincere, or superficial (e.g., actions contradict the emotion displayed; can turn emotions "on" or "off" quickly) or when emotional expressions are used for gain (e.g., emotions displayed to manipulate or intimidate others).

Specify current severity:
Mild: Few if any conduct problems in excess of those required to make the diagnosis are present, and conduct problems cause relatively minor harm to others (e.g., lying, truancy, staying out after dark without permission, other rule breaking).

Moderate: The number of conduct problems and the effect on others intermediate between those specified in "mild" and those in "severe" (e.g., stealing without confronting a victim, vandalism).

Severe: Many conduct problems in excess of those required to make the diagnosis are present, or conduct problems cause considerable harm to others (e.g., forced sex, physical cruelty, use of a weapon, stealing while confronting a victim, breaking and entering).

Criminal Thinking Assessment

The concept of criminal thinking has emerged from the work of Stanton Samenow. *Criminal thinking* can be rated by professional observation using a scale based upon Stanton Samenow's (1984, 1998) breakthrough work summarized in what he calls "17 errors in thinking." Sample inquiries in Samenow's assessment tool include "For each of the following characteristics, please rate (the youth) on the extent to which he/she demonstrates these tendencies or thinking patterns": pride (e.g., refusal to back down, even on little points), victim stance (e.g., conveying a sense of the "poor me" attitude), anger (e.g., using anger to try and control people). A Likert scale was used to assess each thinking error (1 = almost not at all, 2 = some, 3 = half the time, 4 = frequent, and 5 = almost all the time). Assessing criminal thinking patterns using Samenow's (1998) approach has been in clinical use for many years and such patterns are closely correlated with conduct disordered behaviors (Coll, Juhnke, Thobro, & Haas, 2003; Coll, Thobro, & Haas, 2004). Other examples of thinking errors include power tactics, refusing to accept responsibility, and lack of empathy (Samenow, 1984, 1998).

Substance Abuse

There are many effective tools out there to screen for chemical addiction/abuse. I am going to recommend and briefly describe a non-copyrighted and a copyrighted tool and include the non-copyrighted one here. Contrary to popular myth, most youth are surprisingly open about their alcohol and/or drug use (Miller & Lazowski, 2001). While they may initially skew the frequency and intensity of what and how they use, most will admit readily to using if the right questions are asked non-judgmentally.

The CRAFFT Screening Tool

The CRAFFT is a behavioral health screening tool for use with youth under the age of 21 and is recommended by the American Academy of Pediatrics' Committee on Substance Abuse. It

Table A

Samenow's Assessment of Behavior and Thinking Errors (Criminal Thinking)	
Assessed by: _____ For each of the following characteristics, please rate the youth on the extent to which he demonstrates these tendencies or thinking patterns: 1 = not at all, 2 = some of the time, 3 = about half of the time, 4 = frequently, 5 = almost all of the time	
	SCORE
1 Victim stance: "He started it." "I couldn't help it." "You won't give me a chance." Conveys a sense of the "poor me" attitude.	
2 "I can't" attitude: Uses this when he really means "I won't"—a statement of inability which is really a statement of refusal.	
3 Lack of a concept of injury to others: Does not stop to think how his actions will harm others (except physically); no concept of hurting others' feelings, lack of appreciation of emotional anguish caused.	
4 Failure to put himself in the place of others: Demonstrates little or no empathy unless it is to con someone; does not consider the impact of his behavior on other people.	
5 Lack of effort: Unwilling to do anything which he finds boring or disagreeable. Engages in self-pity and looks for excuses. Complains of lack of energy and psychosomatic aches and pains to avoid effort.	
6 Refusal to accept obligation: Says he "forgot" as an excuse. Does not see something as an obligation to begin with; does what he wants and ignores the obligation.	
7 Attitude of ownership: "If you don't give it to me, I'll take it." Expects others to do what he wants and demands of them as though he is asserting his rights. Treats others' property as though it were already his (theft, "borrowing").	
8 Trust (no concept of): Blames everyone else for not trusting him; tries to make you feel as though it is your fault or your problem that you don't trust him.	

9 Unrealistic expectations: Because he thinks something will happen, it must (thinking makes it so). Expects others to fall into line and accommodate his wishes and whims.	
10 Irresponsible decision making: Makes assumptions and jumps to conclusions, without checking out the facts first. Blames others when things go wrong.	
11 Pride: Refuses to back down, even on little points; insists on his point of view to the exclusion of all others; even when proved wrong, clings to his initial position.	
12 Failure to plan ahead or think long range: Failure is not considered unless it is to accomplish something illicit, or else engages in endless fantasies of tremendous success (being a rock star, etc.).	
13 Flawed definition of success and failure: Equates success with being #1 all the time/overnight and equates failure with being anything less than #1 (then considers himself a zero).	
14 Fear of being put down: Feels put down when even the smallest things don't go his way, does not take criticism without flaring up and blaming others. Feels put down when unrealistic expectations are not met.	
15 Refusal to acknowledge fear: Denies ever being afraid, sees fear as weakness. Fails to realize that fear can be constructive.	
16 Anger: Uses anger to try and control people (may take the form of direct threat, intimidation, assault, sarcasm, annoyance). Anger may go underground ("I don't get mad, I get even"). Anger grows like a tumor and spreads— anything or anyone might be a target.	
17 Power tactics: Attempts to overcome others in any struggle, enjoys fighting for power for its own sake (the issue may be secondary), a "high" for him is in overcoming and dominating people.	
Total score	

75–85 = Uses criminal thinking patterns/behavior almost all the time.
60–74 = Uses criminal thinking patterns/behavior frequently.
45–59 = Uses criminal thinking patterns/behavior about half of the time.
25–44 = Uses criminal thinking patterns/behavior some of the time.
< 24 = Uses criminal thinking patterns/behavior very seldom.

Source: Adapted from Samenow (1998).

Youth Comprehensive Risk Assessment: A Clinically Tested Approach for Helping Professionals, © 2017 Taylor & Francis consists of a series of six questions developed to screen adolescents for high-risk alcohol and other drug use disorders simultaneously. It is a short, effective screening tool meant to assess whether a longer conversation about the context of use, frequency, and other risks and consequences of alcohol and other drug use is warranted.

Screening using the CRAFFT begins by asking the adolescent to "Please answer these next questions honestly," telling him/her "Your answers will be kept confidential," and then asking three opening questions.

If the adolescent answers "Yes" to any one or more of the first three questions, the provider asks all six CRAFFT questions (Table 4.2).

The Substance Abuse Subtle Screening Inventory-Adolescent Form

A copyrighted tool, the Substance Abuse Subtle Screening Inventory-Adolescent Form, 2nd edition (SASSI-A2; Miller & Lazowski, 2001), is also very effective. The SASSI-A2 has been shown to be useful in a broad array of contexts, including court systems and mental health settings (Miller & Lazowski, 2001). According to Miller, the creator of this tool, the adolescent

Table 4.2 **The CRAFFT Screening Tool**

CRAFFT is a mnemonic acronym for the first letters of key words in the six screening questions. The questions should be asked exactly as written.

C – Have you ever ridden in a CAR driven by someone (including yourself) who was "high" or had been using alcohol or drugs?

R – Do you ever use alcohol or drugs to RELAX, feel better about yourself, or fit in?

A – Do you ever use alcohol/drugs while you are by yourself, ALONE?

F – Do you ever FORGET things you did while using alcohol or drugs?

F – Do your family or FRIENDS ever tell you that you should cut down on your drinking or drug use?

T – Have you gotten into TROUBLE while using alcohol and drugs?

Source: Adapted from © CHILDREN'S HOSPITAL BOSTON, 2009 (www.ceasar.org).

form of the SASSI was developed for ages 12 to 18. The SASSI-A2 consists of 52 true/false questions and 26 items (0 to 3 scoring format) allowing for self-report of negative consequences of use of alcohol and other drugs. Through research and clinical trials carried out over 16 years (Miller), the test has exhibited greater than 90% accuracy in identifying those with chemical dependency. Miller indicates that items on the SASSI-A2 touch on a broad spectrum of topics seemingly unrelated to chemical abuse, which makes the instrument less threatening to abusers (Coll et al., 2003).

Trauma

Trauma experiences often are at the heart of behavioral problems (Rivard et al., 2003). The commonly accepted understanding of trauma is that it is specific personal experiences of psychological or physical violence, which can include perpetrations of discrimination, sexual abuse, physical abuse, medical maltreatment, and/or witnessing of violence, terrorism, and disasters (Rivard et al., 2003). Manifestations of trauma can be created by day-to-day challenges in the interpersonal realm (e.g., bullying), by genetic and/or physiological conditions, by chronic profound neglect, or by situations that overwhelm the adaptive capacity of an individual (e.g., crippling poverty). Neurobiological research has proven that overwhelming stress, trauma, and neglect impact the parts of the brain that produce thought and memory and have long-term effects on people, especially young people. For example, youth that have been traumatized often habitualize their coping strategies to control intrusive thoughts and feelings by being aggressive and delinquent by sexually acting out, and by abusing alcohol and other drugs (Rivard et al., 2003; Connor, Doerfler, Toscano, Volungis, & Steingard, 2004).

It is a widely understood fact that, without treatment, many youth will often go on to abuse or harm others and become parents that continue the cycle of trauma (Tomlinson, 2008). For example, traumatized males are more likely to have a primary diagnosis of conduct disorder upon entering therapy rather than PTSD (Connor et al., 2004).

A non-copyrighted trauma screening tool developed by the Federal Government is an excellent way to find out the context and extent of trauma a youth may have experienced (Table 4.3). Previous documentation and trust and openness are key in getting answers to these questions, but as with substance abuse, most youth are often relieved that you are getting a bigger picture from them.

A note of caution: These tools assess and screen negative behaviors, attitudes, and experiences. It is important when using them to not lose sight of the strengths that provide a counter-weight to reported problems and challenges. These identified strengths will also often provide the resiliency "traction" needed for youth to improve, as we will see with Eddie.

Eddie

Eddie finds himself in juvenile detention for destruction of property, illegal drug possession, and assault. He is 17 years old and when we check in with him, he has been detained for two months with an additional three to six months to go if he continues to comply with treatment and school. As you can see on the following pages, his conduct disordered behavior score is above the DSM-IV described threshold (3) and he is in the moderate range, his criminal thinking score is 69, indicating he "uses criminal thinking patterns/behaviors frequently." He indicates much substance abuse, answering "yes" to all six screening questions. Eddie also answers "yes" to all 13 trauma-related screening questions. Eddie is alone in the world and he uses his "tough" persona to cope with this reality. Of course taking this persona too far has caused him much trouble and if he continues down this road he will probably land in prison. An asset search revealed that Eddie is now using his time constructively; he is mechanically gifted and has recently been granted the privilege to work on bikes and cars.

Table 4.3 **Trauma Assessment Tool**

	Questions about trauma (from helping professional/parent's knowledge and/or to ask the youth):
1	Were there any significant traumatic events in your family while you were growing up? YES____ NO____ For example, did any of the following events occur in your family: death of a parent or sibling, hospitalization of a parent or sibling, incarceration of a parent or sibling, divorce, or chronic disease? PLEASE NOTE: _____
2	Were you treated harshly as a child? YES____ NO____
3	Did you ever experience physical, sexual, or emotional abuse as a child? YES____ NO____
4	Did you experience inappropriate physical or sexual contact with an adult or person at least five years older than you while you were growing up? YES____ NO____
5	When you were a child, was there violence in your household, such as battering of family members, involving siblings or a parent and his or her partner? YES____ NO____
6	Do you feel that your parents neglected you while you were growing up? YES____ NO____ For example, were there ever periods during which you did not have adequate food, clothing, shelter, or protection by your parents? PLEASE NOTE: _____
7	Did your parents use alcohol or drugs frequently when you were growing up? YES____ NO____

Did you ever use alcohol or drugs with them?

YES____ NO____

When you were growing up, did anyone else in your family use alcohol or drugs?

YES____ NO____

How did their alcohol or drug use affect you as a child?

PLEASE NOTE: _____

8	Have you or has anyone in your family ever been involved with the child protective system (CPS)? YES____ NO____
9	Did you ever live away from your parents? YES____ NO____ Where were the out-of-home placements? PLEASE NOTE:_____
10	Were you ever in foster care? YES____ NO____
11	Were any of your siblings ever in foster care? YES____ NO____
12	When you were a child, were there any periods when you felt unsafe or in danger? YES____ NO____
13	Have you ever felt that abuse or neglect was justified based on your misbehavior or shortcomings? (In other words, did the client feel that the abuse was his/her fault and that he/she deserved it?) YES____ NO____

Source: Adapted from Substance Abuse Treatment for Persons with Child Abuse and Neglect Issues. (2000). Treatment Improvement Protocol (TIP) Series, No. 36. Center for Substance Abuse Treatment. Rockville (MD): Substance Abuse and Mental Health Services Administration (US).

Table 4.4 DSM-V™ diagnostic criteria: Eddie

Conduct disorder

---

1   A repetitive and persistent pattern of behavior in which the basic
    rights of others or major age-appropriate societal norms or rules are
    violated, as manifested by the presence of at least three of the
    following 15 criteria in the past 12 months from any of the categories
    below, with at least one criterion present in the past six months:

Aggression to people and animals
1   Often bullies, threatens, or intimidates others.   **YES**
2   Often initiates physical fights.
3   Has used a weapon that can cause serious physical harm to
    others (e.g., a bat, brick, broken bottle, knife, gun).
4   Has been physically cruel to people.
5   Has been physically cruel to animals.
6   Has stolen while confronting a victim (e.g., mugging, purse
    snatching, extortion, armed robbery).
7   Has forced someone into sexual activity.

Destruction of property
8   Has deliberately engaged in fire setting with the intention of
    causing serious damage.
9   Has deliberately destroyed others' property (other than by fire
    setting).   **YES**

Deceitfulness or theft
10   Has broken into someone else's house, building, or car.   **YES**
11   Often lies to obtain goods or favors or to avoid obligations (i.e.,
     "cons" others).
12   Has stolen items of nontrivial value without confronting a
     victim (e.g., shoplifting, but without breaking and entering;
     forgery).   **YES**

Serious violations of rules
13   Often stays out at night despite parental prohibitions, beginning
     before age 13 years.
14   Has run away from home overnight at least twice while living in
     the parental or parental surrogate home, or once without
     returning for a lengthy period.
15   Is often truant from school, beginning before age 13 years.   **YES**

2   The disturbance in behavior causes clinically significant impairment
    in social, academic, or occupational functioning.   **YES**

3   If the individual is age 18 years or older, criteria are not met for
    antisocial personality disorder.   **NOT APPLICABLE**

Specify whether:

312.81 (F91.1) Childhood-onset type: Individuals show at least one symptom characteristic of conduct disorder prior to age 10 years.

312.82 (F91.2) Adolescent-onset type: Individuals show no symptom characteristic of conduct disorder prior to age 10 years.

312.89 (F91.9) Unspecified onset: Criteria for a diagnosis of conduct disorder are met, but there is not enough information available to determine whether the onset of the first symptom was before or after age 10 years.

Specify if:

With limited pro-social emotions: To qualify for this specifier, an individual must have displayed at least two of the following characteristics persistently over at least 12 months and in multiple relationships and settings. These characteristics reflect the individual's typical pattern of interpersonal and emotional functioning over this period and not just occasional occurrences in some situations. Thus, to assess the criteria for the specifier, multiple information sources are necessary. In addition to the individual's self-report, it is necessary to consider reports by others who have known the individual for extended periods of time (e.g., parents, teachers, co-workers, extended family members, peers).

Lack of remorse or guilt: Does not feel bad or guilty when he or she does something wrong (exclude remorse when expressed only when caught and/or facing punishment). The individual shows a general lack of concern about the negative consequences of his or her actions. For example, the individual is not remorseful after hurting someone or does not care about the consequences of breaking rules.

Callous—lack of empathy: Disregards and is unconcerned about the feelings of others. The individual is described as cold and uncaring. The person appears more concerned about the effects of his or her actions on himself or herself, rather than their effects on others, even when they result in substantial harm to others.

Unconcerned about performance: Does not show concern about poor/problematic performance at school, at work, or in other important activities. The individual does not put forth the effort necessary to perform well, even when expectations are clear, and typically blames others for his or her poor performance.   **YES**

Shallow or deficient affect: Does not express feelings or show emotions to others, except in ways that seem shallow, insincere, or superficial (e.g., actions contradict the emotion displayed; can turn emotions "on" or "off" quickly) or when emotional expressions are used for gain (e.g., emotions displayed to manipulate or intimidate others).   **YES**

Table 4.4 **Continued**

Conduct disorder

Specify current severity:
Mild: Few if any conduct problems in excess of those required to make the diagnosis are present, and conduct problems cause relatively minor harm to others (e.g., lying, truancy, staying out after dark without permission, other rule breaking).

Moderate: The number of conduct problems and the effect on others intermediate between those specified in "mild" and those in "severe" (e.g., stealing without confronting a victim, vandalism).   **YES**

Severe: Many conduct problems in excess of those required to make the diagnosis are present, or conduct problems cause considerable harm to others (e.g., forced sex, physical cruelty, use of a weapon, stealing while confronting a victim, breaking and entering).

Source: Reprinted with permission from the Diagnostic and Statistical Manual of Mental Disorders, Fifth Edition (Copyright © 2013). American Psychiatric Association. All Rights Reserved.

Table 4.5 **Samenow's Assessment of Behavior and Thinking Errors: Eddie**

Samenow's Assessment of Behavior and Thinking Errors (Criminal Thinking)	
Assessed by: _____ Helping profession _____	
For each of the following characteristics, please rate the youth on the extent to which he demonstrates these tendencies or thinking patterns:	
1 = not at all, 2 = some of the time, 3 = about half of the time, 4 = frequently, 5 = almost all of the time	
	SCORE
1 Victim stance: "He started it." "I couldn't help it." "You won't give me a chance." Conveys a sense of the "poor me" attitude.	3
2 "I can't" attitude: Uses this when he really means "I won't"—a statement of inability which is really a statement of refusal.	3
3 Lack of a concept of injury to others: Does not stop to think how his actions will harm others (except physically); no concept of hurting others' feelings, lack of appreciation of emotional anguish caused.	3

4 Failure to put himself in the place of others: Demonstrates little or no empathy unless it is to con someone; does not consider the impact of his behavior on other people.	3
5 Lack of effort: Unwilling to do anything which he finds boring or disagreeable. Engages in self-pity and looks for excuses. Complains of lack of energy and psychosomatic aches and pains to avoid effort.	4
6 Refusal to accept obligation: Says he "forgot" as an excuse. Does not see something as an obligation to begin with; does that which he wants and ignores the obligation.	4
7 Attitude of ownership: "If you don't give it to me, I'll take it." Expects others to do what he wants and demands of them as though he is asserting his rights. Treats others' property as though it were already his (theft, "borrowing").	4
8 Trust (no concept of): Blames everyone else for not trusting him; tries to make you feel as though it is your fault or your problem that you don't trust him.	5
9 Unrealistic expectations: Because he thinks something will happen, it must (thinking makes it so). Expects others to fall into line and accommodate his wishes and whims.	5
10 Irresponsible decision making: Makes assumptions and jumps to conclusions, without checking out the facts first. Blames others when things go wrong.	4
11 Pride: Refuses to back down, even on little points; insists on his point of view to the exclusion of all others; even when proved wrong, clings to his initial position.	5
12 Failure to plan ahead or think long range: Failure is not considered unless it is to accomplish something illicit, or else engages in endless fantasies of tremendous success (being a rock star, etc.).	5
13 Flawed definition of success and failure: Equates success with being #1 all the time/overnight and equates failure with being anything less than #1 (then considers himself a zero).	4
14 Fear of being put down: Feels put down when even the smallest things don't go his way, does not take criticism without flaring up and blaming others. Feels put down when unrealistic expectations are not met.	4

Table 4.5 **Continued**

15 Refusal to acknowledge fear: Denies ever being afraid, sees fear as weakness. Fails to realize that fear can be constructive.	5
16 Anger: Uses anger to try and control people (may take the form of direct threat, intimidation, assault, sarcasm, annoyance). Anger may go underground ("I don't get mad, I get even.") Anger grows like a tumor and spreads—anything or anyone might be a target.	5
17 Power tactics: Attempts to overcome others in any struggle, enjoys fighting for power for its own sake (the issue may be secondary), a "high" for him is in overcoming and dominating people.	3
Total score	**69**

75–85 = Uses criminal thinking patterns/behavior almost all the time
60–74 = Uses criminal thinking patterns/behavior frequently.
45–59 = Uses criminal thinking patterns/behavior about half of the time.
25–44 = Uses criminal thinking patterns/behavior some of the time.
  < 24 = Uses criminal thinking patterns/behavior very seldom.

Source: Adapted from Samenow (1998).

Table 4.6 **The CRAFFT Screening Tool: Eddie**

CRAFFT

C – Have you ever ridden in a CAR driven by someone (including yourself) who was "high" or had been using alcohol or drugs? **YES**

R – Do you ever use alcohol or drugs to RELAX, feel better about yourself, or fit in? **YES**

A – Do you ever use alcohol/drugs while you are by yourself, ALONE? **YES**

F – Do you ever FORGET things you did while using alcohol or drugs? **YES**

F – Do your family or FRIENDS ever tell you that you should cut down on your drinking or drug use? **YES**

T – Have you gotten into TROUBLE while using alcohol and drugs? **YES**

Source: Adapted from © CHILDREN'S HOSPITAL BOSTON, 2009 (www.ceasar.org).

Table 4.7 **Trauma Assessment Tool: Eddie**

	Questions about trauma (from helping professional/parent's knowledge and/or to ask the youth):
1	Were there any significant traumatic events in your family while you were growing up? YES _X_ NO____ For example, did any of the following events occur in your family: death of a parent or sibling, hospitalization of a parent or sibling, incarceration of a parent or sibling, divorce, or chronic disease? PLEASE NOTE: **Drug abuse**
2	Were you treated harshly as a child? YES _X_ NO____
3	Did you ever experience physical, sexual, or emotional abuse as a child? YES _X_ NO____
4	Did you experience inappropriate physical or sexual contact with an adult or person at least five years older than you while you were growing up? YES _X_ NO____
5	When you were a child, was there violence in your household, such as battering of family members, involving siblings or a parent and his or her partner? YES _X_ NO____
6	Do you feel that your parents neglected you while you were growing up? YES _X_ NO____ For example, were there ever periods during which you did not have adequate food, clothing, shelter, or protection by your parents?
7	Did your parents use alcohol or drugs frequently when you were growing up? YES _X_ NO____

Table 4.7 **Continued**

	Did you ever use alcohol or drugs with them? YES **X** NO____ When you were growing up, did anyone else in your family use alcohol or drugs? YES **X** NO____ How did their alcohol or drug use affect you as a child? Scared
8	Have you or has anyone in your family ever been involved with the child protective system (CPS)? YES **X** NO____
9	Did you ever live away from your parents? YES **X** NO____ (Where were the out-of-home placements? PLEASE NOTE: **Foster home, juvenile detention**
10	Were you ever in foster care? YES **X** NO____ (List out-of-home placements: 2 placements)
11	Were any of your siblings ever in foster care? YES **X** NO____ (sister)
12	When you were a child, were there any periods when you felt unsafe or in danger? YES **X** NO____
13	Have you ever felt that abuse or neglect was justified based on your misbehavior or shortcomings? (In other words, did the client feel that the abuse was his/her fault and that he/she deserved it?) YES **X** NO____

Source: Adapted from Substance Abuse Treatment for Persons with Child Abuse and Neglect Issues. (2000). Treatment Improvement Protocol (TIP) Series, No. 36. Center for Substance Abuse Treatment. Rockville (MD): Substance Abuse and Mental Health Services Administration (US).

Let's pick up with Eddie talking with a counselor supervisor about his progress to date, two months into his placement in juvenile detention. The counselor supervisor is helping the counselor specifically identify how Eddie is indicating trauma and what criminal thinking patterns are coming through that will possibly make it challenging to proceed in a productive manner (Table 4.8).

Table 4.8 **Session with Eddie**

C = Counselor E = Eddie	Trauma indicated	Criminal thinking indicated
C: I'd like to know what you're thinking career-wise.		
E: I want to work with Mercedes Benz, then I want to open up my own little shop. I think I can do that without going to training school. I'm a good mechanic.		#9 Unrealistic expectations
C: I heard you are a good mechanic. It sounds like you think you can jump right in to working as a mechanic at a Mercedes Benz shop. E: Yeah, Mercedes or Lexus or whatever. Doesn't really matter. I'll go anywhere. I really don't have any ties.		
C: So you'll go anywhere. How do you get there from here? E: I don't know, asking for help I guess, which I really don't like to do 'cause I like to do stuff on my own.		#12 Failure to think ahead #11 Pride
C: You don't like to ask for help, and sometimes you have to. E: It's hard, yeah. I really don't want relationships with a lot of people out there. Most can't be trusted and just tend to piss me off.		#16 Anger #8 Trust
E: I guess I don't trust much because of being beat up some in my family. C: You really feel pissed off just thinking about it. E: Oh yeah.	#3 Physical abuse	#8 Trust

Table 4.8 **Continued**

C = Counselor E = Eddie	Trauma indicated	Criminal thinking indicated
C: How'd it work out? E: I went to foster care after one bad scene 'cause I did not want to go home, but my parents didn't really like that idea. I figured I'd just go to foster care for six months to a year and then go home but it didn't work out cause of their drinking. I don't talk about my parents a lot.	#7 Parents frequently using substances #9 Living away from parents	
C: It's hard to talk about, think about. E: Yeah, I don't want to think about it at all.		
E: If I think about my past, it's going to slam me down. I don't want that to happen.		#15 Refusal to acknowledge fear
C: Ok, let's go back to what you've got going now? E: Well, when I get out of here, I'll have my own apartment, I'm looking forward to that.		#9 Unrealistic expectations
C: How will you get there? E: I don't know, probably have to ask for help again.		#12 Failure to plan ahead
C: I understand you need to pay back $1000 for destruction of property as restitution. E: Yeah with my bike fixing business, I'm down to $700.		
C: That's great. E: Don't like to talk with counselors much. You haven't been bad, but just so you know.		#12 Failure to plan ahead #8 Trust
E: I might say the wrong thing and I'll get more issues put on me—I just don't want to do that, I want to be in and out of here as fast as possible. I don't want to think about some of the things that happened to me in my past, I just want to think about my future—because my past is done and over with, I have no desire to think about it.	Trauma indicated	

C: You're worried you might say   #8 Trust
   something that will keep you here
   longer.
E: Yeah.
C: So it's like you have to be careful.
E: Yeah.

C: You're probably feeling some of that now.

E: Yeah, I like to talk to my peers better   #17 Power
   than older people, I just like to talk   tactics
   with them 'cause they are in my age
   group, that's why they have better
   input. There's nothing wrong with
   adult input, it's just not my preference.
C: Some adults have used what you say
   against you.
E: Some, yeah—they have.

Note that in this conversation, we are able to discern a number of entrenched criminal thinking patterns, such as unrealistic expectations, anger, and refusal to acknowledge fear, all getting in Eddie's way in going forward in a productive manner. A bright spot is that he is willing to discuss his traumatic past to some degree and acknowledge his feelings to some extent. This is a very good sign as better emotional identification and regulation is key if Eddie is to break his destructive patterns, behavior, and thinking, and realize his dreams and plans.

The professional research is clear that exposure to dysfunctional environments during critical periods of development in emotional awareness, expression, and behavior regulation increases the likelihood of maladaptive behaviors and attitudes (Buist, Dekovic, Meeus, & Van Aken, 2004; Cole & Deater-Deckard, 2009; Zegers, Schuengel, Van IJzendoorn, & Janssens, 2008). Certainly this is true for Eddie. For youth with traumatic histories, emotional experiences that are not modulated through cognitive processing (thinking first) are often expressed as maladaptive conduct disordered behaviors (Scott & Resnick, 2009; Taylor & Bagby, 2004).

The two treatment approaches that have great track records for unlocking emotional identification and expression are motivational enhancement and trauma-focused cognitive-behavioral therapy.

Motivational Enhancement (Miller & Rollnick, 2002)

This form of treatment is counselor skill driven and is designed to identify the client's motivations for change and use them to progress through treatment and the change process. The goal is to especially assist the client to find ways to develop internal motivators (their reasons) for change, particularly related to interactions of feelings, thoughts, and behaviors.

This approach involves the following:

1   Helping the person talk
2   Expressing empathy
3   Using open-ended questions
4   Using paraphrasing
5   Affirming the person
6   Using the clients' resistance to illustrate further need for change, through skills such as:
    a   simple reflections
    b   reflection with amplification
    c   rolling with resistance.

Trauma-Focused Cognitive-Behavioral Therapy (TF-CBT, Medical University of South Carolina, 2005)

This treatment modality is designed to help the client address the bio-psychosocial needs of individuals who have experienced significant traumatic events and who also may be experiencing symptoms of PTSD.

Some of the common forms of trauma clinically proven to be treated effectively through TF-CBT are:

•   sexual abuse or rape
•   physical abuse

- mental abuse
- experiencing or witnessing traumatic events
- any other forms of trauma.

Therapeutic Components

1 Establishing and maintaining a therapeutic relationship
2 Psycho-education about childhood trauma and PTSD
3 Emotional regulation skills
4 Individualized stress management and relaxation techniques
5 Connecting thoughts, feelings, and behaviors to past trauma events
6 Assisting the client in developing and sharing a narrative about the traumatic event(s)
7 Processing and clarifying the traumatic events with client and parent(s) as appropriate.

Let's now shift to three months later with the same counselor supervisor checking in on Eddie after an intentional implementation of these therapeutic concepts. Let's follow along as the counselor supervisor engages with Eddie and reinforces components from both therapeutic modalities with particular focus on how his emotional identification and expression are improving.

Chapter Summary

Eddie's problems were systematically identified through using assessments and the helping professional(s) working with him to effectively delve below the surface of his difficult behaviors and attitudes, to identify feelings, and connect them to thoughts and behaviors, and to appropriately talk about the trauma he suffered. The assessment tools provide necessary insight into Eddie's issues and the appropriate application of the motivational and trauma interventions delivered a winning combination of helping Eddie better identify and regulate his emotions to break out of his destructive patterns.

Table 4.9 **Session with Eddie (three months later)**

C = Counselor *E = Eddie*	*Building motivation for change*	*Trauma-focused cognitive-behavioral therapy*
C: Talk to me about how the experience has been for you here the last couple of months.	#1 Helping client to talk	
E: It's been alright. I've gotten more help than in my previous placements. I'm just about done with my GED. The rest is alright. The staff's OK. The counselors are OK. I'm better than I used to be about asking for help. C: Tell me more about that.	#1 Helping the client to talk #6c Rolling with resistance	#1 Establishing a therapeutic relationship
E: I've been in counseling pretty much all my life and I haven't liked counselors bringing stuff from the past that I don't want to talk about. C: So you don't like counselors in the past pushing you to talk about stuff you didn't want to talk about.	#2 Expressing empathy #6c Rolling with resistance	#1 Establishing a therapeutic relationship
E: Yeah. C: That was upsetting to you and it maybe made you nervous? E: Yeah, and the (Child Protection Services—CPS) had counselors there and that's when I remember I had a bad experience.	#2 Expressing empathy	#5 Connecting thoughts, feelings, and behaviors to past trauma events
C: How did they try to get you to talk about stuff? E: Well, when I first got here I was talking to my case manager and he asked some questions about doing any drugs and alcohol, and I said yeah but I've been off drugs for about two years and I've been dry for about nine months and after that he said I had to go to a group to keep	#3 Using open-ended questions	#6 Assisting the client in developing and sharing a narrative about the traumatic event(s)

sober and I had to talk about my trauma. I don't like to be forced to talk about it.

C: That felt like you're being violated, traumatized again and that brings back a lot of anxiety.

E: Yeah. That gets me angry and I resent that.

#2 Empathy (communicating understanding)

#5 Connecting thoughts, feelings, and behaviors to past trauma events

C: You get angry and defensive and that can lead to you shutting down and acting out.

E: Yeah, I was so upset, I went back and picked a fight with another kid.

#3 Using open-ended questions

#5 Connecting thoughts, feelings, and behaviors to past trauma events

C: You see how your feelings connect with your behavior on that one.

E: Yeah, I'm trying to get past this being a problem—I know what to do, what not to do, and I feel confident, I can just remind myself that I need to get control of my feelings.

#4 Using paraphrasing
#3 Using open-ended questions

#5 Connecting thoughts, feelings, and behaviors to past trauma events

C: How is that working? Can you give me an example?

E: Yeah. I've gone two months now without fighting, stealing, any of that stuff. When I'm feeling angry, overwhelmed, I can identify it better and go do deep breathing, find someone to talk to instead of just picking a fight or getting that person back by stealing something from them. This kid in my pod was cursing me and in my face, usually I'd just punch him, but I walked away and was able to go to the bathroom and calm down. By the time I came out, staff had him and it was all over. I felt like saying "dude, you need to get control of your feelings"— something people were saying to me three months ago ...

Table 4.8 **Continued**

C: Wow, what a great example. It sounds to me you've got great insight and made tremendous improvements since the last time we talked. How do you think that's happened?	#5 Affirming #3 Using open-ended questions	
E: A little bit at a time. I learned to manage my feelings a lot better and to stop and think. This improvement makes me feel confident and more in control.		
C: These are some very positive feelings you identified.	#6a Handling resistance through simple reflection	
E: Yeah, when (regular counselor) and I talk, I just take in her input and think about it and come back—I guess it's working.		
C: Even though you haven't liked asking for help in the past.		
E: Yeah, I'm not saying I love it but it's been OK.		
C: So tell me about your plans with career and owing that restitution money.	#5 Affirming	#7 Processing traumatic events
E: I'm on a good start, I got some help and am now accepted into an auto mechanic training program here in town and I have housing till I complete it. I even applied for a scholarship with some help and got it. I have been paying down the $1000 with my work on bikes around here—just about $100 left. You know, I think I just let my stuff that happened with my parents get me down too much; it really helps to talk about it these last couple of months.		
C: That is fantastic and great insight. Congratulations!		

Indeed, after much hard work (another two months in juvenile detention and weekly counseling), Eddie was able to succeed in his specific plans and is now working as a mechanic at a local dealership and living on his own. While the dealership is not Mercedes or Lexus, he seems happy to work on less ostentatious vehicles (Fords), for now.

References

American Psychiatric Association. (2013). *Diagnostic and statistical manual of mental disorders* (5th ed., text rev.). Washington, DC: American Psychiatric Association.

Buist, K.L., Dekovic, M., Meeus, W.H., & Van Aken, M.A. (2004). Attachment in adolescence: A social relations model analysis. *Journal of Adolescent Research, 19*(6), 826–850.

Cole, P.M., & Deater-Deckard, K. (2009). Emotion regulation, risk and psychopathology. *Journal of Child Psychology and Psychiatry, 50*(11), 1327–1330.

Coll, K.M., Juhnke, G.A., Thobro, P., & Haas, R. (2003). A preliminary study using the Substance Abuse Subtle Screening Inventory-Adolescent Form (SASSI-A) as an outcome measure with youth offenders. *Journal of Addictions and Offender Counseling, 24,* 11–22.

Coll, K.M., Thobro, P., & Haas, R. (2004). Relational and purpose development in youth offenders. *Journal of Humanistic Counseling, Education, and Development, 43,* 41–49.

Connor, D.F., Doerfler, L.A., Toscano, P.F., Volungis, A.M., & Steingard, R.J. (2004). Characteristics of children and adolescents admitted to a residential treatment center. *Journal of Child and Family Studies, 13*(4), 497–510.

Miller, D., Trapani, C., Fejes-Mendoza, K., Eggleston, C., & Dwiggins, D. (1995). Adolescent female offenders: Unique considerations. *Adolescence, 30*(118), 429–435.

Miller, F.G., & Lazowski, L.E. (2001). *The Substance Abuse Subtle Screening Inventory for Adolescents* (2nd ed.). New York, NY: Guilford Press.

Miller, W.R., & Rollnick, S. (2002). *Motivational interviewing: Preparing people for change.* New York, NY: Guilford Press.

Rivard, J.C., Bloom, S.L., Abramovitz, R., Pasquale, L.E., Duncan, M., McCorkle, D., & Gelman, A. (2003). Assessing the implementation and effects of a trauma-focused intervention for youths in residential treatment. *Psychiatric Quarterly, 74*(2), 137–154.

Samenow, S.E. (1984). *Inside the criminal mind.* New York, NY: Times Books.

Samenow, S.E. (1998). *Before it's too late.* New York, NY: Times Books.

Scott, C.L., & Resnick, P.J. (2009). *Applied criminal psychology: A guide to forensic behavioral sciences.* Springfield, IL: Charles C. Thomas Publisher.

Substance Abuse Treatment for Persons with Child Abuse and Neglect Issues. (2000). Treatment Improvement Protocol (TIP) Series, No. 36. Center for Substance Abuse Treatment. Rockville (MD): Substance Abuse and Mental Health Services Administration (US).

Taylor, G.J., & Bagby, M.R. (2004). New trends in alexithymia research. *Psychotherapy and Psychosomatics, 73*(2), 68–77.

TF-CBT, Medical University of South Carolina (2005), https://tfcbt.musc.edu.

Tomlinson, P. (2008). Assessing the needs of traumatized children to improve outcomes. *Journal of Social Work Practice, 22*(3), 359–374.

Zegers, M.A., Schuengel, C., Van IJzendoorn, M.H., & Janssens, J.M. (2008). Attachment problem behavior of adolescents during residential treatment. *Attachment & Human Development, 10*(1), 91–103.

Zoccolillo, M., & Rogers, K. (1991). Characteristics and outcome of hospitalized adolescent girls with conduct disorder. *Journal of the American Academy of Child & Adolescent Psychiatry, 30*(6), 973–981.

PART II
TRAJECTORY AND MATURATION

5

THE YCRA

Putting It All Together

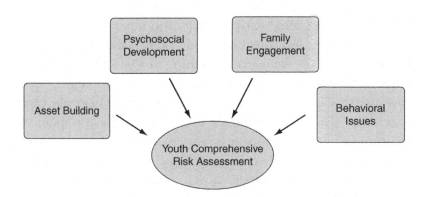

Development of a Comprehensive Risk Assessment Process

In Chapters 1–4, we looked at key YCRA components and their usefulness, and then connected the results with real adolescents to effective interventions. Now I will describe how all of this information can be put together into a powerful comprehensive view. Indeed, comprehensive assessment is considered a recommended best practice for effectively assessing youth (Coll, Stewart, Juhnke, Thobro, & Haas, 2009; Lyons, Kisiel, Dulcan, Cohen, & Chelser, 1997). Stated another way, although each of the assessments and interventions described in Chapters 1–4 were very effective, a more comprehensive approach is even more powerful.

The genesis of the YCRA started over 20 years ago with the professional staff at an adolescent treatment facility. As an outside consultant, I began helping the staff to investigate the presence of common factors among adolescent clients who failed to successfully complete their treatment programs. Case reviews suggested that the most prominent prediction factors for program failure included high runaway risks, multiple prior placements, aggression, substance use, and poor family resources.

On the basis of these early findings and literature recommendations for more individualized and comprehensive assessment (Lyons et al., 1997), we began instituting more formal assessment procedures as part of the treatment process. Increased early assessment efforts at admission were designed to ascertain those areas where youth were the most troubled. Efforts also included discerning who needed longer treatment, required greater supervision, and posed a higher risk to self and others. Additionally, it was hypothesized that these efforts would help predict which youth would improve better and/or faster in treatment, and what additional information might be needed about each youth to further enhance treatment efficacy. Treatment staff have historically disagreed on who was "more troubled or less troubled," thus creating clinical discrepancies and inconsistencies. Therefore, again consistent with suggestions from the professional literature about the importance of discerning frequency and intensity of risk factors, I developed a comprehensive identification process that became the YCRA. This identification process was deemed important by the facility leadership because not only did staff often disagree on treatment approaches, as well as on which youth were at higher risk, needed more help, or functioned most poorly, state and national certifying/accreditation bodies were demanding more specific accountability.

To this end, self-report instruments were selected to be included in a comprehensive assessment, including the Asset Checklist, the MPD (Measure of Psychosocial Development), and the FACES III (Family Adaptability and Cohesion Scales; Olson, 1986). Additional clinical judgment information was gathered at admission and included the presence of any conduct disorder behaviors (APA, 2000) and the extent of criminal thinking patterns, which was based on Samenow's (1998) 17 errors of criminal thinking behavior. The CRAFFT (to ascertain presence of substance abuse) and the Trauma Assessment Tool were added later as we worked to refine the YCRA. Instruments used in this investigation adhered to Coll et al.'s (2009) recommendations that youth assessment processes include both sound clinician-rated measures and client-completed measures. This group of assessments and the protocol followed in the administration and interpretation of the total package became a comprehensive risk factor and social functioning summary called the Youth Comprehensive Risk Assessment (YCRA). See Table 5.1 for an overview of the instrument.

The YCRA was submitted and approved as a performance measurement system with The Joint Commission (TJC) (formerly the Joint Commission on the Accreditation of Healthcare Organizations, JCAHO) (1998). Per TJC approved definition, the YCRA is a clinical assessment process utilized to systematically gather information and make clinical judgments related to six risk areas: (a) risk to self (including risk for suicide, self-harm, becoming a victim, and risk taking); (b) risk to others (including aggression, sexually inappropriate behavior, and destruction of property); (c) social and adaptive functioning (including developmental disorders, handicaps, cognitive disorganization, and social skills); (d) substance abuse/dependency; (e) family resources; and (f) degree of structure needed (frequency of out-of-home placements and need for supervision) (see Table 5.1). Subscales and individual items from the assessments are used to determine scores in five of the six areas (risk to self, risk to others, social and adaptive functioning, substance abuse/dependency, and degree of structure needed). The FACES III and historical/anecdotal information were used to measure the level of family resources.

Table 5.1 **Overview of the YCRA**

Six risk factor areas

1 Risk to self (including risk for suicide or self-harm, risk taking, and risk for victimization)

2 Risk to others (including aggression, sexually inappropriate behavior, and destruction of property)

3 Social and adaptive functioning (including developmental disorders, handicaps, cognitive disorganization, and social skills)

4 Substance abuse/dependency (including attitudes regarding chemicals)

5 Family resources (including family's ability to meet child's needs)

6 Degree of structure needed (including frequency of out-of-home placements and need for supervision)

The YCRA uses a non-equal interval Likert scale of 1 to 4×2 (8), with 1 being slight, 2 being mild, 3 being moderate and 4×2 (8) being severe and requiring immediate treatment interventions.

Supporting assessments for the YCRA
Client-completed measures = MPD, FACES III, Asset Checklist
Clinician-rated measures = Conduct Disorder Behavior Checklist, Criminal Thinking Assessment, Trauma Assessment Tool, CRAFFT

Did You Know?

The YCRA has significant utility in assessing entering adolescent offenders for substance abuse. The results of a recent study suggest that adolescent offenders who score high on the YCRA for substance abuse may well have other risks that are more severe and that require immediate attention. *Higher substance abuse is significantly associated with such factors as risk to self and social and adaptive functioning.* These results suggest that many of these youths are self-medicating due to very poor coping skills and are in desperate need of help. Hence, *by reducing depression and despair, increasing social skills, and improving family relations, treatment programs can promote greater recovery from substance abuse and/or addiction.* Gender-related results suggest that girls are initially more open to admitting substance abuse and personal character defects; however, they are more self-critical. Conversely, boys seem to initially admit less substance abuse and are less self-critical (Coll, Juhnke, Thobro, & Haas, 2003).

Putting It All Together

My minimal assessment timeline for the YCRA process is two 1.5 hour sessions. In this process, I am looking for: (1) areas of strength (AOS) and (2) areas that need improvement (ANI).

In the first session, during the first 45 minutes, I explain the assessment process to the youth. The youth completes the Asset Checklist, MPD, and FACES III, and I ask interview-style questions per the CRAFFT and the Trauma Assessment Tool. I also ask the youth pertinent questions about tendencies and behaviors related to conduct disordered behaviors, criminal thinking, and trauma. In the next 20–30 minutes, I explain the assessment process to the parent(s) or caregiver. They then complete the FACES III. I also ask the caregiver pertinent questions about the youth's tendencies and behaviors as related to conduct disordered behaviors, criminal thinking, and trauma, and for any previous evaluations done with the youth. In the final 15 minutes, I bring the youth and caregiver together to discuss any questions, and I explain the nature of our next meeting.

Chris (an Example)

For simplicity sake, let's assume the previous clients discussed in Chapters 1–4 are now one youth and all client and clinician assessments are completed (see Chapters 1–4). Let's also assume that person's name is "Chris."

To summarize, Chris has completed the Asset Checklist (Chapter 1), Measure of Psychosocial Development (Mary's in Chapter 2), and FACES III (Karl's in Chapter 3). Then clinicians working with Chris have completed the conduct disorder and criminal thinking checklists, the CRAFFT substance abuse tool, and the Trauma Assessment Tool (Chapter 4). Chris's mother completed the FACES III (see Chapter 3) and provided input about Chris.

Now let's plug it all in to the YCRA matrix for a deeper and more comprehensive look at Chris and how to best help him.

Table 5.2 **Chris (scores from actual youth illustrated in previous chapters)**

ASSESSMENT FACTORS *Place appropriate score in corresponding box* *1 = slight risk, 2 = some risk,* *3 = moderate risk, 4 ×2 = severe risk*	NOTES	SCORE *(Note: All scores of 4 are weighted by 2)*

A *RISK TO SELF*
1 Suicide/self-harm
  a No on 2 or more positive identify items scores (Qs 37–40) on Asset Checklist – **Yes**
  b Score of 14 or less on the Asset Checklist – **Yes**
  c Score less than 10th percentile or lower on MPD's Despair – **Yes**
  d Other pertinent information: None
	Further investigate possible depression immediately	If all items No then 1. If any Yes but under 3 Yes, then 3. If 3 or more Yes, then **4×2**.

2 High risk-taking behaviors
  a Yes on Question 14 (has run away) of Behavioral (Conduct Disordered) Checklist?
  b No to Question 32 ("I am good at planning ahead") on Asset Checklist? – **Yes**
  c Yes to any "Serious Violation of Rules" section of Behavioral Checklist (#15) – **Yes**
  d Thinking score +44 – **Yes** (69)
  e Other info (describe):
		If all No, then 1.
		If 1 Yes, then 2.
		If 2 Yes, then 3.
		If 3 or more Yes, then **4×2**.

3 High risk for victimization
  a Yes on Question 13 (stays out all night) of Behavioral Checklist?
  b Has been a victim of physical and/or sexual abuse? (See Q3 of Trauma Tool) – **Yes**
  c 3 or more "yes" on Trauma Tool? – **Yes**
  d Yes to 2 or more items on the CRAFFT – **Yes**
		If all No, then 1.
		If 1–2 Yes, then 2. If 3 Yes, then 3. If 4 or more Yes then **4×2**.

e Other info (describe)? **Yes** –
   has started three fights in last
   three months and been
   injured in all three

Total for RISK TO SELF section   **SCORE = 24 out
                                                  of a possible 24**

B RISK TO OTHERS AND PROPERTY

1 Aggression	Monitor treatment	If all No then 1.
a Yes on 2 or more items on	milieu to protect	If any Yes but
"aggression to people and	all from fighting	under 4 Yes,
animals" section of		then **3**. If 4 Yes,
Behavioral Checklist		then 4×2.

b Lacks concept of injury to
   others (low empathy – 4 or 5
   on Qs 3 and 4 of Behavior
   and Thinking Errors
   Checklist)?
c Thinking score at least +44 –
   Yes (69)
d Score of 2 or more "No" on
   Asset Checklist (Items
   26–30)? **Yes** (3)
e Other info: **Yes** – frequently
   picks fights

2 Sexually inappropriate behavior	If all No then **1**.
a Score on item 7 ("forced	If any Yes but
someone into sexual activity")	under 2 Yes,
on Behavior Checklist?	then 3. If more
b Other info:	than 2 Yes, then
	4×2.

3 Destruction of property/non-	If all No then 1.
interpersonal aggression	If any Yes but
a Score on items 8–15 per	under 3 Yes,
Behavior Checklist (= 2 or	then 3. If 3 or
more within the last year)?	more Yes, then
Yes	**4×2**.

b Thinking score at least +44 –
   Yes (69)
c Other info: **Yes** – threw a
   chair through a window two
   months ago

**Total for RISK TO OTHERS
section**   **SCORE = 12 out
                                                  of a possible 24**

Table 5.2 **Continued**

C *SOCIAL AND ADAPTIVE FUNCTIONING*

1 School functioning
  a Asset Checklist 21–25 (no to
  2 or more)? **Yes**
  b No to either Question 5 or
  Question 12 or both on Asset
  Checklist?
  c 10th% or below on MPD
  intimacy and/or initiative
  and/or industry scales – **Yes**
  d Other info:
	Get permission to
	review recent
	school records
		If all No then 1.
		If any Yes but
		under 3 Yes,
		then **3**. If 3 or
		more Yes, then
		4 × 2.

2 Physical handicap/medical
  maintenance
  a Has medical or physical
  needs requiring increased
  need for supervision and
  structure (enuresis,
  encopresis, asthma, somatic
  tendencies, seizure disorder,
  eating disorder)?
  b Other info:
		If all No then **1**.
		If any yes, but
		under 2 Yes,
		then 3. If more
		than 2 No, then
		4 × 2.

3 Cognitive disorganization/poor
  reality testing
  a Disorganization or confusion
  about what is real versus not
  real?
  b Thinking score at least +44 –
  Yes (69)
  c Other info:
		If all No then 1.
		If any Yes but
		under 2 Yes,
		then **3**. If more
		than 2, then
		4 × 2.

4 Social interpersonal skills
  a Asset Checklist – Questions
  32–36 (2 or more, No) – **Yes**
  b Score of 2 or more on
  Aggression section?
  c Score No on 2 or more of
  Asset Checklist (items 17–20)
  – **Yes**
  d Thinking score +44 – **Yes** (69)
  e 10th percentile or below in
  intimacy and/or trust – **Yes**
  f Other info:
		If all No then 1.
		If any Yes but
		under 2 Yes,
		then 2. If 2 Yes,
		then 3. If 3 or
		more Yes, then
		4 × 2.

Total for SOCIAL/ADAPTIVE FUNCTIONING section   **SCORE = 15 out of a possible 32**

D SUBSTANCE ABUSE

a Abuse and/or misuse of drugs and alcohol within the last year (per CRAFFT)? – **Yes**

b Yes on Trauma tool Q7 (parents)? – **Yes**

c A score of 3 or more on CRAFFT? – **Yes**

d No for Question 31 "important to be use" of Asset Checklist – **Yes**

e Other info:

Immediately refer for more substantive substance abuse assessment

If all No then 1. If any Yes but under 3 Yes, then 3. If 3 or more Yes then **4 × 2**.

E FAMILY RESOURCES

a FACES: Cohesion score? Under 32? – **Yes** (22)

b Trauma total score of 5 or more? – **Yes**

c No on 2 or more items on Asset Checklist? (Questions 1, 2, 6, 11, 14, 16)? – **Yes**

d Other info:

Immediately investigate safe living environment and abuse reporting

If all No then 1. If c (only) is Yes, then 3. If less than 31 on FACES, then **4 × 2**.

F DEGREE OF STRUCTURE

1 Intensity of interventions

a Previous placements and/or outpatient counseling or therapy for family or child? Trauma tool Q9 – **Yes**

b Involvement with therapeutic in-home services, foster care, runaway shelter, day treatment, partial hospitalization, or group home? And/or placement in residential treatment centers, inpatient acute care psychiatric hospitalization, or juvenile correctional facilities? (Q10 on Trauma Tool) – **Yes**

c Other info:

If all No then 1. If a is Yes but not b, then 3. If b is Yes, then **4 × 2**.

Table 5.2 **Continued**

2 Frequency of placements	If all No then 1.
a Prior number of out-of-home	If a is Yes but
placements (one or more)? –	under 2 priors,
Yes	then 3. If more
b Out-of-home placements at	than 3 for a,
an increasingly higher level	and/or b is Yes,
of intensity (e.g., foster	then **4×2**.
home, detention,	
hospitalization) (Q9 and 10	
on Trauma Tool)? – **Yes**	
c Other info:	
3 Need for supervision	If all No then 1.
a Two or more on Aggression	If any Yes but
section of Behavior Checklist?	under 2 Yes,
b Runaway history? (Yes to	then **3**. If more
Question 14 on Behavior	than 3, then
Checklist)	4×2.
c No score on 2 or more on	
Asset Checklist (Items 3, 4, 7,	
8, 9, 10, 13, 15) **Yes**	
d Other info:	
Total Score for DEGREE OF	**SCORE = 19 out**
STRUCTURE section	**of a possible 24**
TOTAL YCRA SCORE	**SCORE = 86**

Note
Do not reproduce this form without the expressed written permission from the publisher.

YCRA Reporting and Interpretation

Reporting and interpretation should be done in the second session, usually a week or two after the first session. The first 30 minutes should be with the youth, then 20 minutes with both the youth and the caregiver to outline agreed-upon goals. In explaining the results, it is important to make sure the youth and caregiver have an understanding of areas of strength (AOS) and areas for improvement (see Table 5.3). It is also important to receive a commitment from the youth to continue to grow strengths and to work on areas for improvement. The caregiver should specifically commit to supporting and helping as directed by the clinician.

Did You Know?

The YCRA has high utility in distinguishing important youth risk patterns. In a recent study, *higher risk youth* (see checklist below) were reported to have significantly more problems with *social functioning* and *substance abuse* and needed a significantly *higher degree of structure* in treatment.

They also exhibited a significantly *higher risk to self and to others* (Coll et al., 2009).

Higher/Lower Risk Identification Checklist

A four-point checklist specifically noted:
1   a high chemical abuse profile

2   the number of conduct disordered behaviors within the last three to six months equal to or greater than three

3   criminal thinking score of "at least half the time" based on Samenow's thinking errors (1–5 scale), and

4   a "disengaged" cohesion score of 31 or below.

Youth Comprehensive Risk Assessment (YCRA)

Chris's overall score of 86 indicates *substantial* and *serious* at-risk behaviors requiring a structured and supervised treatment environment to address his psychological, social, and developmental needs. Recommended treatment priorities include working with Chris's strengths, reduction of *Risk to Self*, especially self-harm, *Risk to Others*, especially destruction of property and/or non-interpersonal aggression, *Social/Interpersonal Skills*. Reducing risk for *Substance Abuse* and increasing *Family Functioning* (e.g., family conflict resolution, communication, and boundary setting) are also high priorities.

Those scoring in this range (about 80% of youth score *lower* in comparison with over 700 tested to date) frequently need *at least 3–6 months of intensive treatment* before being able to successfully move to a less structured and supervised setting. (Note: Information is based only on information provided; some pertinent information may be missing.)

Possible priority treatment goals—see highlighted areas below. Prepared by:

Kenneth M. Coll, PhD

Licensed Clinical Professional Counselor (LCPC), Master Addictions Counselor (MAC)

Note: For more information about the YCRA assessment process and its validity and reliability, go to www.youth riskassessment.com.

Treatment Priorities

Areas of strength: Use Asset Checklist to build current strengths (i.e., support from family) and potential assets (e.g., constructive use of time, empowerment) and commitment to learning.

Areas for improvement: Use Change Plan Worksheet (see page 103, Chapter 6) to prioritize goals.

Did You Know?

The YCRA is useful for outcome evaluation. For example, a recent study indicated that youth from an accredited treatment center made significantly more treatment progress. Even though the youth from a Joint Commission (TJC) accredited site began treatment with significantly higher risk in four of the six YCRA areas, they were at significantly lower risk than the non-TJC youth in the areas of risk to self, social/adaptive functioning, substance abuse risk, and family resources. Intentionality of treatment using the YCRA was indicated as one of the reasons for these dramatic post-treatment differences (Coll & Haas, 2013).

Risk assessment and level of care recommended: Explore Level IV based on information provided.

Score range (recommended):
  1–21 = Level 1 (community-based services, outpatient
          therapy, etc.)

Table 5.3 YCRA summary: Chris, age 15

Risk to self	Risk to others	Social and adaptive functioning	Substance abuse	Family resources	Degree of structure
Range of scores 3–24 (total score = 24/24)	Range of scores 3–24 (total score = 12/24)	Range of scores 4–32 (total score = 15/32)	Range of scores 1–8 (total score = 8/8)	Range of scores 1–8 (total score = 8/8)	Range of scores 3–24 (total score = 19/24)
Self-harm = 8/8 ANI: thoughts of self-harm	Aggression = 3/8 AOS: able to manage emotions	School functioning = 3/8 AOS: motivated to engage in school	**Substance abuse = 8/8 ANI: heavy abuse**	**Family resources = 8/8 ANI: indicated mom engaged but much conflict presently**	Intensity of interventions = 8/8
Risk-taking behavior = 8/8 ANI: will take potentially dangerous risks	Sexually inappropriate behavior = 1/8 AOS: no sexual acting out	Medical maintenance = 1/8 AOS: no medical issues			Frequency of placements = 8/8
Risk for victimization = 8/8 ANI: puts self in harm's way frequently	**Destruction of property and/or non-interpersonal aggression = 8/8 ANI: engages in criminal activity frequently**	Poor reality testing = 3/8 AOS: has some insight			Need for supervision = 3/8 AOS: reasonably (mostly) able to manage emotions and behavior
		Social/interpersonal skills = 8/8 ANI: exhibits poor interpersonal skills			

Total YCRA score = 86

Notes
AOS = area of strength; ANI = area needs improvement.
Bolded areas are suggested immediate treatment priorities.

22–36 = Level II (intensive outpatient therapy)

37–57 = Level III (group home, crisis center, residential treatment program)

>58 = Level IV (psychiatric hospital, residential treatment program, detention facility)

Chapter Summary

The YCRA can be a roadmap to treatment and further assessment, but one note of caution is that the YCRA is not the end all; more information is often needed to support findings, especially in areas such as risk to self, and alcohol and other drugs.

References

American Psychiatric Association (2000). *Diagnostic and statistical manual of mental disorders* (4th ed., text rev.). Washington, DC: American Psychiatric Association.

Coll, K.M., & Haas, R. (2013). Rural adolescent residential treatment facilities as centers of clinical support and excellence. *Advances in Applied Sociology, 3*(2), 102–105.

Coll, K.M., Juhnke, G.A., Thobro, P., & Haas, R. (2003). A preliminary study using the substance abuse subtle screening inventory-adolescent form (SASSI-A) as an outcome measure with youth offenders. *Journal of Addictions and Offender Counseling, 24,* 11–22.

Coll, K.M., Stewart, R.A., Juhnke, G.A., Thobro, P., & Haas, R. (2009). Distinguishing between higher and lower risk youth offenders: applications for practice. *Journal of Addictions & Offender Counseling, 29*(2), 68–80.

Lyons, J.S., Kisiel, C.L., Dulcan, M., Cohen, R., & Chelser, P. (1997). Crisis assessment and psychiatric hospitalization of children and adolescents in state custody. *Journal of Child and Family Studies, 6*(2), 2–18.

Olson, D.H. (1986). Circumplex model VII: Validation studies and FACES III. *Family Process, 25*(3), 337–351.

Samenow, S.E. (1998). *Before it's too late.* New York, NY: Times Books.

PART III

CONTEXTUAL ISSUES

6

MOTIVATION AND READINESS FOR CHANGE

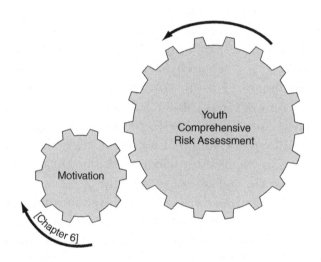

Key Learning Concepts
- Motivational interviewing
- Finding readiness for change: The Change Plan Worksheet
- Illustrative examples with supporting materials

For the purpose of our discussion, *motivation* is defined as the desire to make a behavioral change and *readiness to change* is defined as the acceptance that (typically) professional help can work (Miller & Rollnick, 2002). As the figure introducing this chapter illustrates, motivation is one of the drivers for youth to make improvements by increasing resilience and reducing risks via the YCRA.

In this chapter, I want to provide more detail on typical motivators for struggling youth and introduce the Change Plan Worksheet (CPW) (Miller & Rollnick, 2002). The CPW is a useful tool to discover how ready youth are to make change. As Miller and Rollnick (2002) assert in their research on motivational interviewing (MI), if a problem is not recognized or "owned" by the client (youth), there is no use working on it. An introduction to MI is in Chapter 4. To reiterate, MI is a client-centered, directive method for enhancing intrinsic motivation to change by exploring and resolving ambivalence, and was developed approximately 20 years ago by William Miller (Miller & Rollnick, 2002) to primarily treat problem drinking. However, over the years, research has shown MI to be particularly useful in treatment of youth considered to be difficult, resistant, and/or unmotivated (Miller & Rollnick, 2002). The stakes are high because "unmotivated" youth need help for severe problems while in the midst of a critical stage of psychosocial development, as discussed in Chapter 2, but are unsure about how, where, or whether or not to get help.

Thus, helping professionals must ensure that they are asking the right questions. Miller and Rollnick (2002) remind us that MI is first about the helping professional's attitude, and that MI is *not* about:

- "The youth doesn't see the problem; therefore, I must give them insight" or
- "The youth doesn't understand the problem; therefore, I must give them knowledge" or
- "The youth doesn't know how to change; therefore, I must give them skills" or
- "The youth doesn't care; therefore, I must make them care (by perhaps scaring them)."

The goal of MI is to enhance *readiness for change* through empowered exploration of what the youth wants to work on. MI is accomplished by eliciting the youth's own intrinsic motivations for change, through collaboration, support, empathy, and honoring client autonomy, and through helping youth understand their own motivations (Miller & Rollnick, 2002). The CPW is the critical vehicle for asking the right questions and enhancing the understanding (both client and helping professional) of specific readiness for change. See below.

The CPW asks for information in six areas:

1   The changes I want to make are:
2   The reasons why I want to make these changes are:
3   The steps I plan to take in changing are:
4   The ways other people can help me are:
5   I will know that my plan is working if:
6   Some things that could interfere with my plans are:

In a comprehensive study I conducted with two outstanding doctoral students, Ann Trotter and Stephanie Powell, we adapted the CPW questions to explore the responses of over 51 youth labeled "unmotivated" as determined by professional staff. We extensively interviewed each of the 51 youth over a six-month period in a special program providing "last chance" therapeutic services before entering restricted juvenile detention. These youth were all male, mostly ethnically white (90%) and spanned from ages 13 to 17 years. The questions were asked openly and neutrally, and responses were recorded verbatim. When a youth was uncertain how to answer or was silent, the interviewer was encouraged to clarify. Note: to our surprise, all youth provided a response; if not initially (79% of the youth responded to all questions without prompting), then after a clarifying question was asked (21% responded without prompting).

An important note is that we specifically clarified youth ownership of the change. For example, one youth said, "I want my dad to pay more attention to me." Instead of a response like "Good luck with that," the interviewer clarified possible actions the youth could "own" toward this goal. For example, "talk to my dad about spending more time together," or "first work on my confused feelings about my dad." Note of caution: for some youth, moving through all questions in one setting is unrealistic. Pacing is key; yet it is important to not get too bogged down with one question. The answers to all six questions will form the basis for the critical change work ahead.

CPW Question 1: The Changes I Want to Make Are

It is important to note that a youth with high substance abuse may often pick another area to initially work on. If the helping professional rejects the youth's area—for example, relationships with family—before dealing with substance abuse, resistance often occurs. Using the CPW can be seen as respectively entering a room the youth is inviting you into, and over time the other (perhaps), more critical doors will open.

Utilizing content analysis from our interviews, we were able to discern *five pervasive themes* for question 1 that encompassed all responses. (The changes I want to make are:)

1   Decrease my negative behaviors (31.0% of the respondents)
2   Manage my emotions and thinking better (22.6% of the respondents)
3   Improve my relationships (family) (20.2% of the respondents)
4   Develop positive plans for a better life (14.3% of the respondents)
5   Look to future education goals/employment (11.9% of the respondents)

The results here are encouraging; almost a third of the youth admitted that they wanted to make change concerning their negative behaviors, and another quarter wanted to manage their emotions and their thoughts better. Improving their relationships seems to also be a strong motivator, with life planning and school/academic goals less so, at least initially.

The results show that when approached openly, youth who were labeled "unmotivated" proved indeed to be motivated in specific areas they chose. They were encouraged to be in control of building a plan they could own to promote their own change. As many youths noted, via CPW questions, when their change goals were chosen for them, there was an "un-readiness" to change. With the start of an "owned" plan, we have the beginnings or real *readiness to change.* Let's continue this approach for each of the other five questions to dig into the texture of responses and themes. I will include the percentage responses from the previous question to further highlight patterns.

CPW Question 2: The Reasons I Want to Make These Changes Are

Five pervasive themes for question 2 (reasons) to change:

1 To improve my relationships (29.7%) (20.2% in Q1)
2 To get positive plans for a better life (25%) (14.3% in Q1)
3 To stay out of trouble/jail/prison/leave treatment (20.3%)
4 Because I'm tired of my current behavior (14.1%)
5 To get on with education or employment (10.9%)

Question 2 further promoted ownership in change by reinforcing the payoffs hoped for. Helping professionals can key in on these payoffs and monitor progress toward them. Being tired of the same old behavior and results, as noted with WDEP (Chapter 3), is recognized here. Notice two of the themes in question 1 appeared here as well—improving relationships and trying to build a better life.

CPW Question 3: The Steps I Plan to Take in Changing Are

Question 3 attempts to get at the specific actions to be taken and begin to assist the helping profession in identifying what steps to try *now.*

The *five pervasive themes* from Question 3:

1 Begin first with positive planning for a better life (34.8%) (14.3% in Q1; 25% in Q2)
2 Begin first with learning how to manage emotions and cognition (26.1%) (22.6% in Q1)
3 Begin future school/academic/employment (avoid legal problems) (16.3%) (11.9% Q1; 10.9% Q2)
4 Start to improve relationships by... (16.3%) (20.2% in Q1; 29.7% in Q2)
5 Start to decrease negative behaviors by... (6.5%) (31.0% in Q1)

We are beginning to see patterns now where youth are motivated across common themes. Note the emergence of improving relationships, future education/employment, and positive plans as powerful motivators and a readiness to change to get to work on making change.

CPW Question 4: The Ways Other People Can Help Me Are

The power of others in helping youth make change is very apparent here and a very useful therapeutic motivator. This is a good reminder for helping professionals to identify and rely on significant people for helping youth make positive change. One surprise for us was how important extended family was, for this population more relied on their extended family for helping to change than their mom and/or dad.

Five pervasive themes (who can help me):

1 Extended family—grandparents, aunts/uncles, siblings, step parents (32.4%)
2 Staff (school typically), teachers, nurses, counselors (23.5%)
3 Mom and/or dad (20.6%)
4 Friends or peers (14.7%)
5 Non-family or informal supports (e.g., church) (8.8%)

Note: Staff also are quite powerful in this process!

CPW Question 5: I Know My Plan Is Working If

Question 5 is about reality checking, and can be very useful as therapy progresses.

Five pervasive themes:

1 My education and/or employment is improved (23.5%) (mentioned in Qs 1, 2, 3)
2 Relationships, especially family, are better (23.5%) (mentioned in Qs 1, 2, 3)
3 I have specific plans for a better life (19.6%) (mentioned in Qs 1, 2, 3)
4 Current behavior is better (17.6%)
5 Staying out of trouble/jail/prison/leave treatment (15.7%)

So, for example, reduction of negative emotions, a prominent goal in Q1, now morphs into a very practical way to get there.

As before, we are seeing the very strong motivators of improving relationships, developing specific plans to work on, and looking forward to and progress in education/employment.

CPW Question 6: Some Things That Could Interfere With My Plans Are

These areas are what have held change back, so identification here is crucial in creating all important "relapse" plans and traction/ownership to avoid/overcome any obstacles.

Five pervasive themes:

1 Going back to my old habits (39%)
2 Engaging in negative peer interaction (29.2%)
3 Family conflict and/or problems (12.2%)
4 Problems with my employment, education, or housing (12.2%)
5 Giving up/not seeking help (7.3%)

Chapter Summary

What we found as we looked across all the themes were three salient issues:

1 Supports: Many of these youth are motivated to make change, but lack even the most minimal of supports, so they rely heavily on therapeutic staff. Promoting more informal supports is crucial to success long term.

2 Importance of family relationships (pervasive across the questions): Notice how this comes through loud and clear. One chilling fact with many of the youth we interviewed was that they were struggling to get better connected with family members (see Chapter 3). This work, which can be difficult, has to persist. It is often the key to long-term change, and a powerful motivator.

3 Plans: Note the importance of planning owned by the youth. The instillation of hope and helping youth achieve practical attainable goals and objectives is self-reinforcing.

Additional Helpful CPW Materials

We used such outlines over a period of weeks and months to help staff develop very specific plans and track progress for each youth.

Here also is an example of how a CPW might look after multiple conversations and planning with a particular youth.

As you can see, such a plan can be closely monitored monthly, weekly, even daily. The motivational interviewing process is quite powerful for promoting real, owned change. Coupled with the CPW, this process provides a powerful approach to changing youths' lives.

Reference

Miller, W.R., & Rollnick, S. (2002). *Motivational interviewing: Preparing people for change* (2nd ed.). New York, NY: Guilford Press.

Table B

Change Plan Worksheet Outline

1 The changes I want to make are:

   List specific areas or ways in which you want to change.

   Include positive goals (beginning, increasing, improving behavior).

2 The most important reasons why I want to make these changes are:

   What are some likely consequences of action and inaction?

   Which motivations for change seem most important to you?

3 The steps I plan to take in changing are:

   How do you plan to achieve the goals?

   Within the general plan, what are some specific first steps you might take?

   When, where, and how will these steps be taken?

4 The ways other people can help me are:

   List specific ways that others can help support you in your change attempt.

   How will you go about eliciting others' support?

5 I will know that my plan is working if:

   What do you hope will happen as a result of the change?

   What benefits can you expect from the change?

6 Some things that could interfere with my plan are:

   Anticipated situations or changes that could undermine the plan.

   What could go wrong?

   How might you stick with the plan despite the changes or setbacks?

Table C

Change Plan Worksheet Example:
Jimmy, age 16 (YCRA score = 67 with severe scores related to substance abuse, school functioning, family functioning)

---

1 The <u>changes</u> I want to make are:
   a Stop smoking weed
   b Reduce my drinking
   c Be a better older brother

2 The most important reasons <u>why</u> I want to make these changes are:
   a Get out of trouble with probation; avoid dirty urines
   b Take better care of my health
   c Give myself a better chance at life

3 The steps I plan to take in changing are:
   a Keep coming to group and treatment here
   b Give urines to my P.O. every week
   c Spend time each day focusing on my studies
   d Go to my school every day; meet with my teachers, if I'm having problems
   e Stop using crack, one day at a time
   f Avoid hanging out with people who use
   g Go back to church

4 The ways other people can help me are:
   a My P.O. can encourage me when I give clean urine
   b My counselor can help me deal with my depression and ADHD
   c My group can help me talk about my difficulties
   d My mom can help me with homework

5 I will know that my plan is working if:
   a I am not using weed
   b I am holding down my part-time job
   c I am coming to group 8 out of 10 times
   d I am spending time each day focusing on my goals—school, work, helping my younger sisters

6 Some things that could interfere with my plan are:
   a If I get sent back to juvenile detention for using
   b If I don't plan ahead
   c If I don't stop hanging with using friends
   d If I quit treatment

7 What will I do if the plan isn't working?
   a Be honest with my counselor and my group and ask for help
   b Make another plan that is better
   c Refuse to let myself feel like a failure

7

DIVERSITY ISSUES

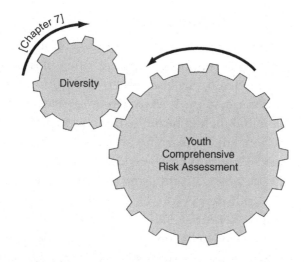

Key Learning Concepts
- Importance of cultural considerations when working with under-represented minority youth from historically oppressed groups
- Examples to illustrate the significance of identity and application of culturally relevant strategies

The importance of cultural considerations in helping understand causation in youth mental health issues is complex, with cultural, social, biological, and psychological factors all contributing (US Department of Health and Human Services, 2001). The most recent Surgeon General's report on mental health indicates that the key considerations of social context,

cultural factors, racism, discrimination, and poverty are
important for understanding contributors to mental health
struggles (US Department of Health and Human Services,
2001). During the past two decades, the federal government,
particularly the Substance Abuse and Mental Health Administration (SAMHSA), has begun recognizing and emphasizing
the importance of culture-based approaches for effective provision of mental health services.

Poverty's Influence

Unfortunately, in our society, lower social economic status and
historically oppressed ethnic groups are often positively correlated (US Public Health Service, 2001), often due to long-term
racism and discrimination. Poverty circumstances all too often
include detrimental mental health experiences, such as actual or
threatened serious injury, learning about unexpected or serious
harm, or death or injury experienced by a family member, abuse,
neglect, domestic violence, and living with an impaired caregiver
(e.g., caregiver with depression, alcohol abuse) (National Child
Traumatic Stress Network, 2004). This kind of social context
presents mental health challenges for youth, in particular and
typically, elevated levels of substance dependence, depression,
stress disorders, disruptive behavior disorders (e.g., conduct disorder and oppositional defiance), phobias, and sleep disorders
(US Department of Health and Human Services, 2001).

Multigenerational Mental Health Issues and Their Consequences

It has long been understood that multigenerational mental
health challenges are often passed on, in that subsequent generations learn from, and are affected by, parents, grandparents, and
other extended family adults, who struggle socioeconomically,
with discrimination, and/or with mental health issues. This phe-
nomenon involves learning to experience feelings such as fear
and helplessness and creating mental health problems (e.g., anger,
depression, and alcohol/drug abuse), through witnessing the

resulting consequences of their attempts to cope with experiences of racism, discrimination, and socioeconomic hardships (Freeman et al., 2016). Stone (2003) and Levine (2001) discuss the long-term effects of mental health challenges of poverty and/or victims of discrimination as often systemic and multigenerational; with continued themes of exaggerated and conflicted feelings of anxiety, panic, and depression in subsequent generations of youth. That being said, it is also important to note that although ongoing oppression and poverty increase vulnerability to mental health problems, we know that many mental health conditions can impact individuals regardless of socioeconomic level (Thomas & Schwarzbaum, 2006).

Promising Practice: Cultural Identity Practices as Protective (Resilience) Factors Against Mental Health Challenges

Thomas and Schwarzbaum (2006) indicate that "personal identity is cultural identity" (p. 1). It is important to note that culture is not just ethnic/racial, as many may unintentionally assume. Thomas and Schwarzbaum (2006) note that "cultural identity and self concept are developed not only within the context of the consciousness of others' perceptions but also within historical images of culture" (p. 4).

> People do not wake up one day and decide to act a certain way. Historical, sociological, anthropological, political, and geographical explanations are needed to make sense of a person's life choices, life cycle events, and patterns of individual and relational behavior.
>
> (ibid., pp. 4–5)

If oppressive historical events are antecedents of mental health problems, some of the solutions to these mental health problems are embedded within that historically oppressed culture and history as well.

Culture in mental health interventions is a complex issue (Moodley & West, 2005), particularly in light of the movement toward science-based (and sometimes culture-free) interventions; however, there are indications that an institutional focus on culture and culturally based interventions, as appropriate, can be key healing factors. Indeed strong cultural identity has been positively correlated with better mental health outcomes (Johnston, 2002; Moodley &West, 2005).

Using the YCRA System to Promote Culturally Relevant Mental Health Practices

Did You Know?

A study using the YCRA compared psychosocial risk behaviors of adolescents who are deaf or hard of hearing with their hearing peers in a mental health treatment facility. Using the YCRA, statistically significant differences emerged between groups (Coll, Cutler, Thobro, Haas, & Powell, 2009).
Key points from an extensive literature review asserted that:

- An alarming number of adolescents who are deaf or hard of hearing are referred to mental health treatment because of perceived difficulties in communication and co-occurring mental health disorders (Zieziula & Harris, 1998).
- Martinez and Silvestra (1995) and McEntree (1993) noted that adolescents who are deaf or hard of hearing are inadequately or inaccurately identified, and are often not provided adequate resources compared to their hearing peers that would have allowed for earlier intervention.
- Utilizing clinical and multi-source information, Luetke-Stahlman (1995) examined emotional and behavioral correlates in a large sample of adolescents and found that the prevalence of psychopathology in adolescents who are deaf or hard of hearing is significantly greater than for hearing adolescents, especially in regard to emotional disorders. Luetke-Stahlman (1995) denoted that interaction among hearing adolescents and those who are deaf or hard of hearing is minimal, and close friendships are rare.
- Individuals who are deaf or hard of hearing identify themselves to be a distinct culture and linguistic minority (Filer & Filer, 2000; Lala, 1998). Martinez and Silvestra (1995) and McEntree (1993) noted that the way in which adolescents who are deaf or hard of hearing examine their cultural identity may lead to internalization of negative stereotypes.
- An unusually high proportion of youth who are deaf or hard of hearing receive mental health treatment (Bat-Chava, 2000; League for the Hard of Hearing, n.d.).

Key results: Overall, the deaf or hard of hearing (*DHH*) group demonstrated significantly higher ratings on measures of *risk to self and others, social and adaptive functioning, need for structure, and aggression.* This study discovered that aggression and assault were significant factors in a majority of deaf adolescents referred for residential treatment, whereas *substance abuse* was a key reason for referral in *hearing adolescents.* The results of this study are also consistent with a growing body of research that indicates the importance of positive *identity formation* in adolescence.

Key conclusions/recommendations for working with deaf or hard of hearing youth in residential treatment:

- Establishing positive cultural identity as early as possible provides a strong foundation for developing quality of life (Coll et al., 2009). Parents who expose children to their culture initiate the process of identity exploration toward a more positive cultural identity. Promoting "deaf culture" as a positive term is indicative of pride and communal identity. Therefore, it is of critical importance for parents and counselors to understand and promote "deaf culture."
- Parent education and family programs provide a context for schools and parents to work collaboratively to promote cultural identity, and reduce the risk of maladaptive behaviors (Bat-Chava, 2000; League for the Hard of Hearing, n.d.).
- Among the biggest indicators of positive deaf cultural identity development is whether adolescents who are deaf or hard of hearing are able to *speak or use American Sign Language* (Filer & Filer, 2000; Lala, 1998).
- Classrooms should be organized to facilitate critical thinking and empowerment. When students are provided opportunities to develop opinions and investigate solutions to problems, they take critical steps toward positive identity formation.
- Therapy should focus on building resilience, promoting positive beliefs though patterns, stress management, decision making, goal-setting skills, fostering positive self-definition, and social skills. It is particularly important to encourage adolescents who are deaf or hard of hearing to challenge the negative beliefs they may have internalized about themselves as individuals with disabilities.
- Aggression should be addressed by emphasizing the basics of rules and structure, and taking measured steps in this process. Specific suggestions for dealing with social adaptive functioning include: (a) role-playing immediately after a deaf youth is observed missing a social cue, (b) using affect identification and regulation techniques (Coll, Thobro, & Haas, 2004), and (c) spending extra time training staff in restraint alternatives and in fostering greater understanding of cultural differences between adolescents who are deaf or hard of hearing and their hearing peers.

An Illustrative Example of a YCRA Outcome-Based Case Study

The American Indian/Alaska Native (AI/AN) populations, in particular, report a high occurrence of such risk factors (Manson, 2001). Beals (1997) compared the mental health disorders of AI/AN youth with those of non-minority children and found that AI/AN youth were more likely to report significantly higher rates of depression, alcohol, and other drug (AOD) abuse, and suicidal acts. Garrett (1999) notes that many of the current problems that the AI/AN populations have with depression and suicidal behaviors can be tied back to historical cultural trauma—most notably, genocide, the land grabs based on the Dawes Act of 1867, the outlawing of Native religions, and the massive federal program designed to relocate reservation Indians to urban areas.

Adolescent offenders in therapeutic communities are to establish specific and integrated individualized treatment based on their AOD abuse, co-occurring with other risk factors (e.g., depression) (Burdsal, Force, & Klingsporn, 1990; Grimley et al., 2000). Bauman, Merta, and Steiner (1999) assert that the first step in treating adolescent AOD abuse is comprehensive risk assessment.

Using the YCRA, we undertook a recent case study. This case study approach was deemed valuable to a youth mental health treatment agency in its effort to determine how to best help AI/AN youth (about 20% of their clients). I was asked to coordinate this case study approach in an attempt to find a clear example that would provide valuable insight to the agency in treating AI/AN youth. The purpose of using this approach was not to offer generalizable conclusions necessarily, but to provide an accounting of the experience and learn from it.

Nancy

Nancy was an American Indian adolescent mandated through the Child in Need of Supervision (CHINS) provision into the mental health treatment program. A clinical treatment team (consisting of the clinical director, myself, the counselor assigned to Nancy for individual and family counseling, and the two counselors to be working with Nancy in group counseling) began gathering information from Nancy. She belonged to a Northern Plains tribe and came from a rural Indian reservation. Her age at admission was 14 years, 6 months. Nancy's grandmother had referred her to the state's Department of Family and Children's Services. Her grandmother reported to the treatment team that Nancy would not get out of bed on most days, was irritable, and was drinking alcohol and smoking marijuana on a regular basis.

YCRA Assessment

Nancy was administered cognitive and academic assessments. Results of an intelligence assessment revealed an above-average IQ, and her academic achievement at a ninth-grade education level. During the first two weeks of Nancy's admission, the treatment team completed the YCRA.

During the initial risk assessment period, Nancy openly discussed with me and other members of the treatment team the fact that over the last year she had been in a group home for three months and had spent two weeks in a psychiatric hospital related to a suicide attempt. In accord with past records, Nancy, during a structured series of interviews using the YCRA, reported that she has a long history of depression, beginning at age seven, and has repeatedly and recently threatened to kill herself. She attempted to hang herself during the last six months. Nancy also discussed having been teased and picked on by American Indian and non-American Indian peers at school—describing comments referring to her as "an Indian from a bad family."

Nancy described her mother (currently serving a long prison sentence) as having a history of severe alcoholism. Nancy had no information about her father other than that he was an American Indian. Nancy revealed that her grandmother has raised her over the last several years in a generally nurturing and supportive environment. Nancy indicated that she gets along well with and is helpful toward her six-year-old sister. Nancy also indicated that her brother died in a car accident last year at the age of 16 years. During the initial assessment phase, Nancy appeared motivated to dig herself "out of this hole, at least for grandma and little sister's sake," and demonstrated sadness about the losses in her life. She cried when discussing her mother, her brother, and how much her grandmother loves and cares about her.

Using the information from Nancy's interview and her YCRA scores, the treatment team developed a treatment plan. The treatment team also requested that I present this information, with Nancy's permission, to professional staff, framing Nancy's issues in a cultural context based on the professional literature when possible.

YCRA Results

Of the six YCRA scales, there were notable elevations related to the Risk to Self scale. This scale includes the categories risk for suicide, self-harm, risk taking, and victimization. It reflects an individual's tendency to put himself or herself in harm's way, by either direct behaviors (e.g., suicide attempts) or indirect behaviors (e.g., AOD abuse).

A moderate risk score on the Risk to Self scale is 9; Nancy's score of 15 was considered very high. As indicated, Nancy entered mental health treatment with an extensive history of depression, including suicide ideation and one significant attempt. She also had significant environmental stressors and serious grief and loss issues (involving her mother and brother). This high Risk to Self score is in keeping with literature regarding the internalization of anger in populations that have been the victims of racism and subsequent trauma (Beiser, 1997). The cycle of racism and trauma suggests that oppression becomes internalized, often due to external messages (Manson, 2001). In many situations, it is viewed as unsafe to express anger toward the dominant culture, so anger is often turned inward (Sue & Sue, 1999).

Nancy showed positive social and adaptive functioning (score = 10). She entered mental health treatment with no extensive risk history in this area. Nancy's lower score on social and adaptive functioning (a score of 15 is average) is consistent with literature on the relational worldview of many tribal peoples (Garrett, 1999). The relational worldview concept accents interpersonal relationships and highly respects responsibility toward others.

Nancy was rated as a very high risk in relation to substance abuse. Risk scores below 3 indicate lower risk. Nancy's Substance Abuse scale score was 8, indicating the highest risk rating. Nancy's responses noted extensive alcohol and other abuse, problems with impulsiveness, low frustration tolerance, detached feelings, and difficulty accepting the significance of substance abuse in her life. Studies show that the use and abuse of alcohol and other drugs to cope with current circumstances and trauma are much more prevalent among American Indian youth than among non-American Indian youth (Hawkins, Cummins, & Marlatt, 2004).

During the initial YCRA assessment period, Nancy was cooperative and indicated that she felt much despair and that life had little meaning. She said she felt sad about her mother and brother and saw little she could do to change things.

Culturally Relevant Treatment

Based on the information gathered, the treatment team directed Nancy to the drug education class, which described the costs of addiction, and to the AOD group, which followed the rudimentary 12-step process. Both the class and the group met weekly for 1.5 hours and were recently infused with content related to other high-risk factors, such as self-harm. Two licensed counselors co-facilitated both the drug education class and the AOD abuse group.

Consistent with the current research base, the weekly one-hour individual counseling sessions with Nancy incorporated motivational interviewing (MI). This individual counseling supported self-efficacy, with Nancy's Change Plan Worksheet (CPW) serving as ongoing follow-up (Miller, 1993). Nancy's goals, as set out on her worksheet, included academic success, social skill development, extended family connecting, and positive peer relationships. The treatment team also developed a plan with the school that encouraged Nancy's involvement in active classroom instruction, emphasized interactive teaching and cooperative learning, and used tutoring.

Other individual counseling goals used to help Nancy deal with her depression and suicidal thinking focused on increasing her sense of self-worth, reducing her isolation, teaching stress management, encouraging better communication and problem-solving skills, and helping promote inner-directedness, through journaling (Jongsma, Peterson, & McInnis, 1996). The agency's psychiatrist determined that Nancy needed psychotropic medication based on a genetic condition and/or early trauma. Such medication has been proven effective with adolescents (Jongsma et al., 1996).

Nancy's social adaptability was noted as a strength on which we could help her build. For example, after encouragement by other treatment team members and me, Nancy decided to volunteer at the school and began tutoring younger residents, with great success.

Nancy's grandmother was included in all decisions about Nancy's treatment plan and was consulted, along with Nancy, via bi-weekly conference calls. This focus is consistent with the recommendations for family-centered treatment of adolescents made by Brendtro, Brokenleg, and Van Bockern (1998) and by Burden, Miller, and Boozer (1996).

Concomitantly and specifically for Nancy, as an American Indian youth, our treatment team and Nancy's grandmother adopted the philosophy that Nancy could be best understood when viewed within her cultural context; of vital importance is that the treatment team questioned Nancy extensively about her wishes concerning culturally specific healing. As Manson

(2001) noted, traditional healing is common in many AI/AN communities, with ethnographic studies indicating that traditional healing does indeed help such problems as depression and substance-related disorders. Moreover, traditional healing approaches frequently operate in cooperation with Western psychotherapeutic interventions (Csordas, 1999; Guilmet & Whited, 1989). The treatment team helped Nancy become involved with traditional healing services from her community. Services that were coordinated by the RTC and accessed by Nancy included sweat lodge purification, smudging, and other ceremonies (e.g., the offering of food).

As a treatment team, we drew on the work of Garrett (1999), who indicated that many AI/AN children tend to define themselves less by possessions and more by family ties and traditional customs and beliefs. He noted that, with such a strong cultural emphasis on one's relationship with others (especially with extended family), AI/AN children are susceptible to encountering a variety of difficulties (including depression and suicidal thinking) often coming into conflict with the larger society that emphasizes individualism, competition, and achievement over contrasting values of group harmony, cooperation, and sharing.

The staff at this facility responded to this knowledge and understanding by promoting and expanding extended family involvement and participation in the development of AI/AN youth. For example, in cooperation with, and with approval from Nancy's tribe, the treatment team added a sweat lodge on-site. A tribal elder is currently coordinating the sweat lodge process. The purpose of the sweat lodge is to cleanse and purify the body, while the prayers heal the spirit.

Nancy was reassessed after six months using the YCRA, and her scores indicated that she had made significant therapeutic progress, with impressive reductions in risk to self, increased social and adaptive functioning, reduced substance abuse risk, and decreased degree of structure. The most notable change for Nancy was in risk to self. In her responses on standardized tests and during her exit interview, Nancy reported a much stronger sense of purpose, much lower despair, less likelihood to act out her depressed feelings, and greater resolution of negative feelings. Nancy indicated that her attitudes and behaviors around substance abuse also seemed to change. She reported more insight about her reasons for using AOD in the past, and she went home on two unsupervised visits and did not use AOD. The tribal elder also reported that Nancy seemed to have a much stronger identity and had new perspectives on what she could give back to her community.

It seemed likely that through cultural and traditional AI connections, and family-centered treatment planning and implementation, Nancy would be able to move home and continue a nurturing relationship with her grandmother and sister. For Nancy, following general treatment best practices and infusing treatment programming with traditional spirituality, language, teachings, and ceremonies (Beiser, 1997; Garrett, 1999) produced a 28-point reduction in overall risk behaviors on the YCRA (from 60 to 32). After she experienced culturally appropriate and family-centered treatment opportunities, Nancy's risk-to-self behaviors and attitudes noticeably decreased, resulting in less treatment time and an appropriate and supportive home placement.

Key Conclusion

Nancy made improvements overall and especially in the area of risk to self, most likely due to the intense involvement of her grandmother in treatment and the specific, culturally sensitive interventions that were employed. AI/AN youth have often been painted in the literature as being "sicker" than non-AI groups (Manson, 2001). From Nancy's results, however, a reasonable conclusion is that, in spite of high risk, this youth was able to make great gains with culturally sensitive treatment. This supports the growing literature emphasizing the strong resiliency of AI/AN populations (Manson, 2001). The treatment team shared these results and recommendations with all professional staff. Consequently, treatment planning for AI youth has incorporated the protocols described with similar promising results.

These positive results suggest the possibility that treatment approaches for AI youth could be adapted to build strength and resiliency for non-AI youth. For example, with group work, the relational worldview could be reinforced as a model for all youth struggling with social skills. The treatment team is now exploring the value of such ideas. Indeed, the YCRA has been implemented with other AI/AN youth, with similar results.

Chapter Summary

It is clear from this example as well as from the "Did you know?" box that cultural considerations and interventions are paramount for influencing change. Cultural identity must be respected and its development encouraged.

References

Bat-Chava, Y. (2000). Diversity of deaf identities. *American Annals of the Deaf*, *145*(5), 420–428.

Bauman, S., Merta, R., & Steiner, R. (1999). Further validation of the adolescent form of the SASSI. *Journal of Child & Adolescent Substance Abuse, 9*, 51–70.

Beals, J. (1997). Psychiatric disorder among American Indian adolescents. *Journal of the American Academy of Child & Adolescent Psychiatry, 36*, 1252–1259.

Beiser, M. (1997). Mental health and the academic performance of first nations and majority–culture children. *American Orthopsychiatric Association Journal, 68*, 455–467.

Brendtro, L.K., Brokenleg, M., & Van Bockern, S. (1998). *Reclaiming youth at risk*. Bloomington, IN: NES.

Burden, C.A., Miller, K.E., & Boozer, A.E. (1996). Tough enough: Gang membership. In D. Capuzzi & D.R. Gross (Eds), *Youth at risk* (2nd ed., pp. 283–306). Alexandria, VA: American Counseling Association.

Burdsal, C., Force, R., & Klingsporn, M.J. (1990). Treatment effectiveness in young male offenders. *Residential Treatment for Children & Youth, 7*, 75–88.

Coll, K.M., Cutler, M., Thobro, P., Haas, R., & Powell, S. (2009). An exploratory study of psychosocial risk behavior of adolescents who are deaf or hard of hearing: Comparisons and recommendations. *American Annals of the Deaf, 154*(1), 30–35.

Coll, K.M., Thobro, P., & Haas, R. (2004). Relational and purpose development in youth offenders. *Journal of Humanistic Counseling, Education and Development, 43,* 41–49.

Csordas, T.J. (1999). Ritual healing and the politics of identity in contemporary Navajo society. *American Ethnologist, 26,* 3–23.

Filer, R.D., & Filer, P.A. (2000). Practical considerations for counselors working with hearing children with deaf parents. *Journal of Counseling and Development, 78,* 38–43.

Freeman, B.J., Coll, K.M., Two Dogs, R., Iron Cloud Two Dogs, E., Iron Cloud, E., & Robertson, P. (2006). The value of Lakota traditional healing for youth resiliency and family functioning. *Journal of Aggression, Maltreatment & Trauma, 25*(5), 455–469.

Garrett, M.T. (1999). Soaring on the wings of the eagle: Wellness of Native American high school students. *Professional School Counseling, 3,* 57–64.

Grimley, D., Williams, C.D., Miree, L.L., Baichoo, S., Greene, S., & Hook, E. (2000). Stages of readiness for changing multiple risk behaviors among incarcerated male adolescents. *American Journal of Health Behavior, 24,* 361–369.

Guilmet, G.M., & Whited, D.L. (1989). *The people who give more: Health and mental health among the contemporary Puyallup Indian tribal community.* Denver, CO: University Press of Colorado.

Hawkins, J.D., Cummins, L.H., & Marlatt, G.A. (2004). Preventing substance abuse in American Indian and Alaska Native youth: Promising strategies for healthier communities. *Psychological Bulletin, 130,* 304–324.

Johnston, S.L. (2002). Native American traditional and alternative medicine. *Annals of The American Academy of Political and Social Science, 583,* 195–213.

Jongsma, A.E., Peterson, L.M., & McInnis, W.P. (1996). *The child and adolescent psychotherapy treatment planner.* New York, NY: Wiley.

Lala, F.J.J. (1998). Is there room in the DSM for consideration of deaf people? *American Annals of the Deaf, 143*(4), 314–317.

League for the Hard of Hearing. (n.d.). *Deaf or hard of hearing population statistics.* Retrieved January 6, 2004, from www.lhh.org.

Levine, J. (2001). Working with victims of persecution: Lessons from Holocaust survivors. *Social Work, 46*(4), 350–360.

Luetke-Stahlman, B. (1995). Social interaction: Assessment and intervention with regard to students who are deaf. *American Annals of the Deaf, 140*(3), 295–303.

Manson, S. (2001). Behavioral health services for American Indians. In Y. Roubineaux & M. Dixon (Eds), *Promises to keep: Public health policy for American Indians and Alaska Natives in the 21st century* (pp. 174–185). Washington, DC: American Public Health Association Publications.

Martinez, M., & Silvestra, N. (1995). Self-concept in profoundly deaf adolescent pupils. *International Journal of Psychology, 30*(3), 305–316.

McEntree, M.K. (1993). Accessibility of mental health services and crisis intervention to the deaf. *American Annals of the Deaf, 138*(1), 26–30.

Miller, W. (1993). *Motivational Enhancement Therapy manual.* Rockville, MD: US Department of Health and Human Services.

Moodley, R., & West, W. (Eds). (2005). *Integrating traditional healing practices into counseling and psychotherapy.* Thousand Oaks, CA: SAGE Publications.

National Child Traumatic Stress Network. (2004). *Core Clinical Characteristics.* CRF Version 3.0 20050922.

Stone, J.B. (2003, March). *Post-colonial stress disorder and post-traumatic stress disorder: Implications for tribal/native substance abuse, mental health, and dual diagnosis assessment and treatment.* Presentation given at the National Indian Child Welfare Association (NICWA) Circles of Care Grantee Meeting, Portland, OR.

Sue, D.W., & Sue, D. (1999). *Counseling the culturally different* (3rd ed.). New York, NY: Wiley.

Thomas, A.J., & Schwarzbaum, S. (2006). *Culture and identity: Life stories for counselors and therapists.* Thousand Oaks, CA: SAGE Publications.

US Department of Health and Human Services. (2001). *Mental health: Culture, race and ethnicity.* Rockville, MD: Author.

US Public Health Service, Office of the Surgeon General. (2001). *Surgeon general report on mental health: Culture, race and ethnicity.* Atlanta, GA: US Department of Health and Human Services.

Zieziula, F., & Harris, G. (1998). National survey of school counselors working with deaf and hard of hearing children: Two decades later. *American Annals of the Deaf, 143*(1), 40–45.

8

PSYCHOTROPIC
MEDICATIONS

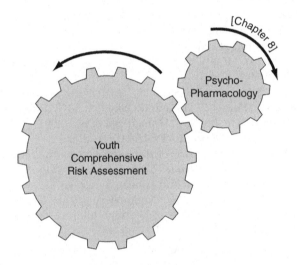

> **Key Learning Concepts**
> - State of affairs for psychotropic medication with youth
> - Illustrative example—YCRA comprehensive report and YCRA baseline and six-month summaries with a youth on two medications

The State of Affairs: Psychotropic Medications With Youth

Average annual growth rates for the prescription of psychotropics to youth in the United States has increased since the 1990s, with especially rapid acceleration after 1999 (Thomas, Conrad, Casler, & Goodman, 2001). This increase may be associated with changing thresholds of diagnosis and treatment, availability of new medications, and changes in federal regulatory policies concerning promotion of medications by the pharmaceutical industry (Thomas et al., 2001).

Only a few psychotropic medications have been approved for use among children younger than 18 years. However, it has become increasingly common to use these medications to treat a variety of mental health disorders among children. Of course, many mental health disorders are first identified during adolescence, and depression is a serious problem in this age group. Current estimates of the prevalence of psychiatric disorders among adolescents who have ever experienced at least one psychiatric disorder has been estimated to be as high as 31% for girls and 42% for boys (Thomas et al., 2001).

Mental health clinicians working with youth often will evaluate youthful offenders presenting problems such as insomnia, depression, disruptive behaviors, or other anxiety, and initiate referrals to psychiatrists for further diagnostic evaluation and possible psychotropic medication treatment. Many youth receiving mental health services are taking multiple medications when initiating therapy, whereas others in need have never received medications; a comprehensive mental health assessment, such as the YCRA, provides an opportunity to help reassess their psychotropic medication and psychiatric referral needs.

Experts agree that, when psychotropic medications are used with youth, they should augment a comprehensive and individually developed mental health treatment plan with the youth's compliance and active participation in individual, group, and family therapy and other appropriate treatment interventions. Clinicians should also implement behavioral interventions and strategies such as regular exercise and improved sleep hygiene, encouragement of available family members and other social supports to rally around a youth, facilitation of additional staff supervision and support, development of additional supportive relationships with both peers and direct care staff, and focus therapy (individual, family, group) on building trust and encouraging identity exploration; it is vitally important that a helping professional consult regularly with the prescribing psychiatrist and that regular meetings take place for monitoring effectiveness, side effects, and eventual withdrawal of use.

Two or More Psychotropic Medications

In recent years, multiclass psychotropic treatment has become increasingly common in the medical care of American children and adolescents. Antidepressant and attention-deficit hyperactivity disorder (ADHD) medication combinations were the most prevalent multiclass psychotropic regimen (Comer, Olfson, & Mojtabai, 2010).

Several possible factors may have contributed to the recent increase in multiclass psychotropic treatment in children's outpatient care. First, greater patient, parent, or physician emphasis on symptoms has contributed to the trend. Second, an increasing number of psychiatrists are specializing in pharmacotherapy (Comer et al., 2010).

The empirical foundations of pediatric psychopharmacology have rapidly expanded during the past two decades as well. Especially promising is a series of randomized controlled trials that documented the short-term efficacy among children and adolescents of psychotropic medications for disorders such as ADHD, obsessive-compulsive disorder, generalized anxiety disorder, and major depressive disorders (Comer et al., 2010).

Psychotropic Medication in Action

We conducted a recent study of 87 youth receiving mental health treatment in a restricted juvenile justice setting, with psychiatric support to ascertain most prescribed drugs. The following tables (Tables 8.1 and 8.2) may be illustrative of general trends in adolescent psychotropic medication. These tables are not meant to be comprehensive.

Table 8.1 **Most common medications (% use includes first or second medication)**

Most common medications utilized:

- Lithium
- Abilify
- Seroquel
- Prozac
- Effexor

78% of youth were prescribed at least one medication; and 56% of the youth were prescribed two or more medications.

Steve

Steve is a typical example of a psychotropic and therapeutic success story. Steve is a 15-year-old male who came into treatment because of a serious suicide attempt. He also has a history of fighting and his parents recently contentiously divorced. Steve's baseline YCRA score was quite high (74) and there were more troubling issues with Steve that clearly pointed toward possible help through psychotropic medication. Given this fact, a very specific comprehensive report was compiled. This kind of report is recommended when clinicians are faced with complex and multiple issues that clearly point to psychotropic medication as a possible aid in conjunction with other therapies.

Youth Comprehensive Risk Assessment Report and Treatment Plan
EXAMPLE (Steve)

Name: _____

Date of placement: _____ Date of assessment: _____

DOB: _____   Adjudication: _____

Referring Agency: _____

Attention: *Juvenile Justice/Dept of Health and Welfare*

Recent history and history of admission: Steve has been having increasing difficulties at home and at school managing his behavior (e.g., explosive behavior) and responding to

124 CONTEXTUAL ISSUES

Table 8.2 **The use and frequency of psychotropic medications**

Psychotropic medications	Generally for treatment of	Prescribed frequency
1 Abilify (aripiprazole)	Anxiety	22.7%
2 Adderall (amphetamine mixed salts)	ADHD	9.8%
3 Benzodiazapam—Anticonvulsive	Aggressive behavior	–
4 Carbamazepine (epitol, tretol)	Bipolar	–
5 Catapres (clonidine)	Pain relief	9.4%
6 Celexa (citalopram)	Depression, bulimia, OCD	3.4%
7 Concerta (methylphenidate)	ADHD	1.4%
8 Depakote (divalproex sodium)	Bipolar	4.3%
9 Desyrel (trazodone)—Deplanx.	Depression	2.9%
10 Dexadrine (dextramphetamine)	ADHD	–
11 Effexor (venlafaxome)	Anxiety, depression	16.1%
12 Haldol—Psychosis	Anxiety, impulsive behavior	–
13 Klonopin (clonazepam)	Anxiety, pain relief	–
14 Lexapro (escitalopram)	Depression	–
15 Limictal (lamotrigine)	Bipolar	11.2%
16 Lithium (Eskalith, Lithobid, Loxitane, Lithonate)	Bipolar, aggression	27.8%
17 Neurontin (gabapentin)	Impulsive behavior	–
18 Orap (pimozide)	Tourette's	–
19 Paxil (paroxetine)	Antidepressant	–
20 Prozac (fluoxetine)	Antidepressant, impulse control	17.9%
21 Risperdal (risperidone)	Bipolar	4.9%
22 Ritalin (methylphenidate)	ADHD	2.0%
23 Seroquel (quetiapine fumarate)	Bipolar, depression	19.2%
24 Strattera (atomoxetine)	ADHD	6.3%
25 Symbyax (fluoxetine/ olanzapine)	Bipolar, depression	–
26 Wellbutrin (bupropion)	Depression, anxiety	13.2%
27 Xanax (alprazolam)	Anxiety, depression	–
28 Zoloft (sertraline)	Antidepressant	4.9%
29 Zyprexa (olanzapine)	Bipolar	6.9%

reasonable requests by his mother and teachers. He was suspended from school for a week and a meeting was held to determine a reasonable treatment option. His parents were unwilling to place him in a therapeutic group home as they had heard about alleged physical abuse that had taken place there. He was admitted to our residential treatment program on ...

Physical/medical assessment: Steve was given a physical examination on ... He was noted to have small bruises on his lower back and chin and an abrasion to his lower lip, which were apparently a result of several restraints and self-harming episodes that occurred during his first few days of placement. He refused to remove any clothing during the examination and refused certain examinations. The medical staff have been unable to obtain a health history yet, as Steve is not a good historian and his cooperation was tenuous. Overall, he appears to be a healthy adolescent boy with no obvious physical problems. He was admitted on the following medication regimen: Depakote (divalproex) 500 mg, tid; Prozac (fluoxetine) 25 mg in the am; and Ativan (benzodiazapam) 0.5 mg, qid; and Ativan 1.0 mg every hour as needed up to three doses in a 24-hour period. The Ativan was discontinued on the day of admission and the Divalproex was also discontinued after two weeks of observation on ..., replaced by a mild dosage of Abilify (aripiprazole). Since this medication adjustment, Steve is much more oriented and cooperative.

Previous diagnosis: (—, L.P.C., date)

Axis I: Oppositional Defiant Disorder
Axis II: No diagnosis
Axis III: No diagnosis
Axis IV: Stressors: problems relating to primary support group and problems relating to authority figures
Axis V: Current GAF = 50

Risk to self-assessment: Using testing instruments, which are primarily self-report and symptom and behavior checklists, revealed that Steve does have some tendencies toward withdrawal and depression, has poor self-esteem, and views himself as being less cooperative and less assertive than his peers. Because of his tendency to view the world egocentrically, he has difficulty empathizing with others and appreciating the impact of his behavior on other people. He also has a tendency to view people dichotomously, as either being good or bad. He appears to harbor a rather negative attitude toward authority and does not feel loved or as belonging to any particular group, including his family. Specifically, his score on the Mood Assessment indicates mild depression. Positive identity items on the Asset Checklist note that he is low in this area. Additionally, assessments of thinking errors show that he is steeped in this kind of thinking (see Criminal Thinking Checklist).

Risk to others assessment: The staff report that Steve has a hard time keeping his room and personal space neat and clean. He demonstrates the ability to do this when reminded, but does not seem to take pride in doing it on his own. He tends to have difficulty handling conflicts and disagreements without becoming aggressive, is not respectful of the needs and boundaries of others, does not seem to consider the consequences of his actions and the impact of his behavior on other people, and has a hard time refraining from annoying and bothering other people, especially when he is agitated. Steve also has a difficult time expressing his emotions, taking responsibility for his behavior, and using unstructured time in a positive fashion. He is generally unwilling to accept the consequences of his behavior, often does not comply with rules, and often has difficulty complying with reasonable requests of the staff.

Steve acknowledges a number of problems, including feeling inferior, being inconsiderate of self and others, resisting authority, leading and following others in negative behavior, annoying and irritating others, making threats and bullying peers, responding with anger at the slightest frustration or challenge, stealing, lying, and putting up a front to keep from showing his true feelings.

Legal assessment: Steve was placed at the Juvenile Detention Center in ... County on two different occasions because of his explosive and self-harming behaviors, when all other possible resources had been exhausted to ensure his safety.

Social and adaptive functioning assessment: Concerning specific developmental problems, Steve was given **educational assessments**. Results of cognitive testing, using the WISC-III, reveal that Steve's verbal IQ is 75, performance IQ is 99, and full scale IQ is 85. A previous evaluation resulted in somewhat lower scores: verbal 67, performance 94, and full scale 78. It was the examiner's opinion that Steve's receptive and expressive command of the English language is below average and that he tends to be quite concrete. He has been attending school at ... Junior High School in ... where he was in the seventh grade. His cumulative GPA is 2.16. His Woodcock-Johnson scores are as follows:

	Age Equiv.	Grade Equiv.
Letter-word ID	8–2	2.9
Reading fluency	9–0	3.6
Calculation	10–1	4.5
Math fluency	11–3	5.9
Spelling	8–9	3.8
Writing fluency	12–7	7.1
Passage comprehension	7–1	1.8
Applied problems	8–4	2.8
Writing samples	7–7	1.9

	Age Equiv.	Grade Equiv.
Broad reading	8–1	2.7
Broad math	9–5	3.9
Broad written language	9–8	4.5
Total achievement	8–9	3.4

In terms of physical handicaps and medical maintenance, none were indicated. For cognitive disorganization and/or poor reality testing, Steve scored moderately. Social interpersonal skills are rated poor. Results from the Asset Checklist (items 17–20, 21–25, 32–36) note that Steve struggles with constructive use of time, school engagement, and a positive identity.

Substance abuse assessment: The results from the adapted CRAFFT indicate the possibility of a substance abuse disorder, although Steve denies use of either drugs or alcohol. His elevated score may indicate lack of insight or understanding about the extent to which his life is dominated by substance use. Considering his denial of any history of drug or alcohol use, this finding must be evaluated in that context. It may be that Steve's receptive language deficits may be interfering with the test results. The presence and/or extent of this problem warrant further evaluation.

Family assessment: Steve was born in ... on ... following a normal pregnancy and delivery. He has been described as a quiet, generally happy child. He reached developmental milestones within normal time frames. His father is 35 years old and is a carpenter. He is not proficient in the English language and this has been a stated source of frustration for Steve. His mother, J... [hereafter, J], is 31 years old and is a waitress. Steve has a younger brother, ..., who is 12 years old, and a much younger sister, ..., who is three years old. J describes the family environment as "stressful" and indicates it is much calmer if the "kids get what they want." J reports that Steve and his brother fight a lot, but that he is more nurturing with his little sister. She says the family enjoys outdoor activities such as camping, hiking, fishing, and biking.

J reports that over the past three to four years, Steve's behavior has become increasingly oppositional, rageful, and uncooperative. He has demonstrated explosive behavior, during which he seems to lose control of himself, which includes throwing things, breaking things, hitting and scratching himself, spitting on others, arguing, lying, and demanding things from others. He has required mechanical restraint at times (in the hospital and at the detention center), and has also been chemically restrained at times. J also reports that as a young child, Steve would "go limp" to demonstrate his oppositionality and unwillingness to respond to his mother's requests. Although J reported viewing this as "normal" childhood oppositional behavior, she indicated that sometimes she thought he screamed more than normal children. When asked if she could identify a particular time in Steve's life when things began to deteriorate, she identified two things that may have been contributory, although she also indicated that she did not remember that things got dramatically worse at these times. When Steve was four or five years old, she and her spouse moved in with his parents in order to save money for a house. J recalled that Steve's grandmother seemed to have more ability to control his behavior, especially at bedtime. She also identified that when she went to work (five years ago) the family schedule was significantly disrupted, and that Steve seemed to respond somewhat negatively to this lack of predictability and structure. Steve reported that, as a young child, he went fishing and hunting with his father and seemed to enjoy these outings. Recently, their relationship had deteriorated, and frequently would involve power struggles resulting in physical altercations.

J reported that approximately six or seven years ago, her brother began staying with them periodically when he was "going through tough times." She said he had been in prison for forgery and since his release has had a hard time keeping jobs and remaining stable, and that he has stayed with them off and on. She reported that Steve's relationship with him seemed positive, but acknowledged that he tended to get into the same types of power struggles with Steve as with his dad, both of them attempting to force Steve to comply, rather than attempting other, more encouraging interventions. When asked if Steve had always displayed the kind of regressive behavior that he now exhibits, she indicated that he had always played with younger kids, thrown temper tantrums, and been somewhat oppositional. Since starting Junior High School, his immaturity seemed more pronounced to J as she noticed that Steve did not enjoy the things his peers were doing (going to the mall, playing sports). J said that Steve had been invited to a couple of birthday parties, but always called and asked to be taken home early in the evening.

J would like to be involved in Steve's treatment program as much as time and distance will allow. The referring agency has made provisions to support this effort financially, and this involvement is strongly recommended.

J completed a family communication and satisfaction inventory, the results of which provide important information about how she perceives the family's problems. Steve reports a lack of physical affection between him and his mother, and says that his mother insults him when she is angry with him. Steve also reports that the family has a hard time solving problems together, and is critical of one another. On the FACES III, Steve's scores suggest that he does feel emotionally bonded with other family members, and the family environment feels chaotic and unpredictable to him.

Degree of structure assessment: Need for supervision as related to intensity of interventions, frequency of placements, and results from the Asset Checklist reveals that it is high at this time.

YCRA summary of recommendations: Utilizing all information from the assessment tools used, background history, and current behavioral observations, a risk factor assessment was completed on ... His score was 74, indicating a need for Level IV (detention/psychiatric) care. This finding reflects the potential that Steve may require psychiatric hospitalization if his behaviors become problematic enough to put him or others at risk of significant harm. His risk for psychotropic medications is likely related to anxiety, and/or aggression toward others. His overall profile is one of a highly distressed treatment resister, based on the fact that Steve does exhibit the risk factors typically seen with residents who are resistant to treatment, such as conduct problems, high levels of social skill challenges, and significant emotional distress. His highest risk factors are in the areas of:

- **Aggression toward others:** Steve demonstrates significant aggression toward other people and property, and does not easily exhibit empathy or remorse for his actions.
- **Family resources:** Although Steve reports some emotional engagement with family members, it appears that there has been considerable conflict between him and his father over the past two years, and he has had a troubled and conflictual relationship with his brother as well. His mother indicates that she doesn't feel she has the resources or understanding of the problem to be able to deal with the situation effectively.
- **Social interpersonal skills:** Steve has a lot of trouble getting along with others, resolving conflict, communicating effectively, and demonstrating empathy. He is easily annoyed and provoked, and provokes and bothers others without cause. He behaves in a child-like, somewhat immature fashion, and can be quite emotionally needy and clingy at times.
- **Suicide/self-harm:** Although Steve denies depression and/or suicidal ideation, his testing suggests that he is experiencing significant psychic distress. He has trouble

sleeping, is bothered by nightmares, and has not been able to talk about the sources of his distress. He also hits and slaps himself, and pulls at his hair when he is upset.

- **Physical/developmental/medical problems:** Steve's IQ has been tested and found to be in the borderline range. He acts younger than his chronologic age, and his behavior is quite regressive at times.
- **Destruction of property/non-interpersonal aggression:** Steve often throws, breaks, and destroys things in his environment when he is angry or aggravated. He demonstrates little ability to control himself when he begins to do this, and shows very little remorse.
- **High risk-taking behaviors/high risk for victimization:** Difficulties with communication and impaired coping and social skills put him at some risk in this area.

Areas of lower risk include:

- **Frequency of placements:** This is Steve's first placement out of the home.
- **Substance use:** No significant history, either in Steve or in family members.
- **Sexually inappropriate behavior:** No history.
- **Cognitive disorganization:** Although Steve demonstrates exceedingly poor judgment, he does not appear to have any thought disorder or disorganization in his thinking processes.

Overall strengths per the Asset Checklist and observations:

- Steve can be very likeable and engaging when he wants to be.
- In spite of the results of his cognitive testing, he appears to be quite bright and curious about things.
- It appears that interpersonal relationships are very important to Steve.

Top priority treatment strategies within the next few months (see treatment ideas, links):

1   Because interpersonal relationships appear to be important to Steve, this may be an effective avenue through which to help him gain **social skills,** empathy, and greater relational awareness of his impact on others.

2   Background information suggests that Steve has always displayed some level of child-like and regressive behavior patterns. A more thorough assessment of his level of **social and adaptive functioning (specific developmental problems)** and capacity for mature behavior and decision making may be helpful in the treatment process.

3   Because he can be so physically **aggressive** and impulsive **(high risk to others)**, a brief time-frame behavioral chart may be helpful and positively reinforcing every effort he makes to self-control.

4   Steve reports that he is unsure of his mother's feelings toward him, which may be an important starting point in **family** therapy because of Steve's strongly negative reactions to perceived rejection by others.

Identified discharge needs: It is somewhat unclear what type of discharge plan will be appropriate for Steve. The course of treatment will hopefully identify his needs and assess his ability to function in a family system to a degree which will promote his social and emotional well-being. It seems evident that he will need ongoing support and assistance with emotional expression, behavior management, and medication monitoring. Whether family reunification is a viable discharge option will be determined within 6–12 months of treatment.

Admission diagnosis: (Dr. —):

Axis I: Oppositional Defiant Disorder, Intermittent Explosive Disorder

Axis II: No diagnosis

Axis III: No diagnosis
Axis IV: Problems with primary support group
Axis V: GAF = 35

Estimated discharge date: Based on his history, circumstances, and resources, and considering the outcome of the risk assessment, it is recommended that Steve's length of placement be 6–12 months.

_____   Date: _____

_____, M.S., L.P.C.

Counselor _____

Verification date _____

Dr. _____

Youth Comprehensive Risk Assessment (YCRA) Summary

After four months, Steve began the process of withdrawing from both medications, while maintaining gains in highlighted areas based on implementation of top priority treatment strategies outlined.

Chapter Summary

Psychotropic medications must be considered as part of best practice in working with youth. The cautions and caveats noted in this chapter must also be considered.

References

Comer, J., Olfson, M., & Mojtabai, R. (2010). National trends in child and adolescent psychotropic polypharmacy in office-based practice, 1996–2007. *Journal of the American Academy of Child & Adolescent Psychiatry, 49*(10), 1001–1010.

Thomas, C.P., Conrad, P., Casler R., & Goodman, E. (2001). Trends in the use of psychotropic medications among adolescents, 1994 to 2001. *Psychiatric Services, 57*(1), 63–69.

Table 8.3 YCRA summary: Steve, age 16; YCRA score baseline: 74; YCRA score at six months: 49

Risk to self	Risk to others	Social and adaptive functioning	Substance abuse	Family resources	Degree of structure
Range of scores 3–24 (total score = 13/24)	Range of scores 3–24 (total score = 17/24)	Range of scores 4–32 (total score = 15/32)	Range of scores 1–8 (total score = 2/8)	Range of scores 1–8 (total score = 8/8)	Range of scores 3–24 (total score = 19/24)
Self-harm = 8/8^ ANI 6mo 3/8	Aggression = 8/8^ ANI 6mo 3/8	School functioning = 3/8 AOS	Substance abuse = 2/8 AOS	Family resources = 8/8 ANI 6mo 3/8	Intensity of interventions = 8/8
Risk-taking behavior = 3/8	Sexually inappropriate behavior = 1/8	Medical maintenance = 1/8			Frequency of placements = 8/8
Risk for victimization = 2/8 AOS	Destruction of property and/or non-interpersonal aggression = 8/8^ ANI 6mo 3/8	Poor reality testing = 3/8			Need for supervision = 3/8 AOS
		Social/interpersonal skills = 8/8^ ANI 6mo 3/8			

Note

^ Medication combination currently is *Ability* for sleep, anxiety, and impulse control (taken at night), and *Prozac* for depression and aggression (taken in the morning).

HELPING THE HELPERS

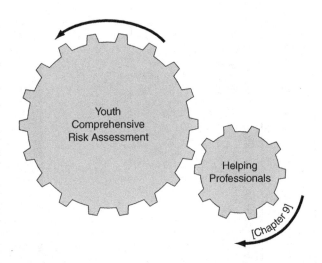

Youth
Comprehensive
Risk Assessment

Helping
Professionals

[Chapter 9]

Key Learning Concepts
- Long-term challenges facing helping professionals working with demanding youth with YCRA admission scores of +60
- An illustrative example outlining assessment and interventions

The Challenge

Helping professionals working with youth who have serious mental health issues are faced with many professional challenges (McWhirter, McWhirter, McWhirter, & McWhirter, 2007). Unfortunately, many helping professionals tend to have little training in specialized youth diagnosing, intervening, and treating of mental illness; meanwhile, the need grows exponentially (Lyons, Kisiel, Dulcan, Cohen, & Chelser, 1997). Compared to many adult settings (e.g., private practice, insurance payer), settings dealing with high-risk youth (e.g., residential treatment, juvenile justice, intensive outpatient) consistently report higher incidences of burnout and related problems (Maslach, Jackson, & Leiter, 1981).

While there are many benefits to counseling in youth settings, such as sharing in sometimes incredible individual and family changes, varied tasks and functions, and community identity and recognition, youth mental health professionals often face role overload, heightened stress and burnout, relationship/role/boundary problems, and economic issues (i.e., scarcity of resources). This reality is often exacerbated by the challenges of working with bureaucratic systems (e.g., child protection services, courts) (Coll & Haas, 2013).

In various studies, my colleagues and I have found that the major challenges discussed by youth mental health counselors who are working with the most challenging youth (e.g., YCRA scores of +60) are often limited resources, few staff members with large caseloads, very challenging presenting client issues (e.g., physical, sexual abuse), limited supervision and consultation options, and high employee turnover (Coll & Haas, 2013). As we all know, a professional cannot be helpful if they themselves are fatigued and impaired.

An Illustrative Example

Mary

Mary works at an adolescent residential treatment facility as the counselor for 15 youth in a "home group" called a cottage and has come for professional consultation and coaching in a professional crisis. Mary is 41 years old. She has been working with youth at her agency for eight years. She has a Masters in Counseling and is European American.

Individualizing Next Steps

I used four assessment tools with Mary I have found helpful with professionals in Mary's situation. Her presenting problems were feeling overloaded, ineffective, exhausted, and "at her wits end." The instruments I utilized were as follows:

1 A 17-item survey in which the items were derived primarily from prior helping professional function and professional development research and literature (piloted with youth mental health counselors) was used to measure job functions and professional development activities (Coll & Freeman, 1997; Coll & Rice, 1993).

2 The Maslach Burnout Inventory (MBI), developed by Maslach, Jackson, and Leiter (1981), includes three scales: *emotional exhaustion* measures feelings of being emotionally overextended and exhausted by one's work; *depersonalization* measures an unfeeling and impersonal response toward recipients of one's service, care treatment, or instruction; and *personal accomplishment* measures feelings of competence and successful achievement in one's work (Maslach et al., 1981). The Maslach consists of 22 items on a 1–6 Likert scale.

3 The Role Questionnaire (RQ) was used to measure role conflict and consists of 8 items on a 1–7 Likert scale. The RQ specifically measures role conflict related to internal standards, external expectations, heavy role demands, conflicting responsibilities, and incompatible requests from others (Coll & Freeman, 1997). Construct validity for the RQ has been verified through factor analysis and proven across several samples, factor and scale analysis was later substantiated, and internal reliability for numerous groups was measured at 0.75 (Coll & Rice, 1993). The RQ has been used by teachers, high school supervisors, special education teachers, manufacturing supervisors, foremen, salespersons, clerical staff, nurses, public utility workers, hospital staff, and hospital aides (Coll & Rice, 1993).

4 The Measurement of Psychosocial Development (MPD) that readers are familiar with from Chapter 2 is an Eriksonian-based instrument that provides a measure of the positive and negative attitudes associated with each of the eight developmental stages, the status of conflict resolution at each stage, and an index of overall psychosocial health. The MPD is useful in this setting, as it is utilized in a variety of clinical, counseling, training, and research settings because interpretation focuses on youth or adult healthy personality development and growth, instead of pathology (Hawley, 1987).

Mary's Assessment Results

1 Results about job functions indicated that Mary spends most of her time performing record keeping, individual counseling, and crisis intervention (Table 9.1). She noted that she prefers less time on record keeping and administrative tasks and in staff meetings, and more time performing counseling and receiving clinical supervision (Table 9.2).

The record-keeping burden is often high with the most at-risk youth, as there may be county and state social workers assigned to each youth, as well as other community professionals (e.g., school, mental health agencies) to coordinate with. Mary had no idea she spent almost 10 hours per week on record keeping. Indeed it was possible for Mary to reduce her time in this activity so she could increase counseling and supervision. With some brainstorming, she was able to delegate appropriately to an administrative assistant and campus intern to cut her record-keeping hours to five.

2 Burnout information for Mary is mixed. The MBI revealed that she is well above the national norm group for emotional exhaustion scores, but within the average range for depersonalization and personal accomplishments (Table 9.3).

Table 9.1 **Average weekly hours by job function**

Mary's job function	Average hours per week
Presentations	0.5
Record keeping	9.3
Consultation	1.2
Individual counseling	10.5
Group and/or family counseling	2.1
Testing/other duties	3.1
Clinical supervision	1.6
Administration tasks	3.8
Staff meetings	3.0

Table 9.2 **Preferences for job functions**

Mary's job function	I want more	I want less	I'm OK with this as is
Presentations			YES
Record keeping		YES	
Consultation			YES
Individual counseling	YES		
Group and/or family counseling	YES		
Testing/other duties			YES
Clinical supervision (receiving)	YES		
Administrative tasks		YES	
Staff meetings		YES	

I accessed the YCRA scores for the current 15 adolescents Mary was working with at the time. It turns out that 12 of the 15 had YCRA scores of +60 with a median score of 63.5 in her cottage. It also turns out that the Risk to Others scores were significantly higher than the reset of campus, with scores averaging 14 of 24 compared to 8 of 24. This translates into a great deal of acting out behaviors, and projecting of negative feelings onto others (e.g., aggressiveness, bullying, fighting). This information alone was a revelation to Mary and helped her see that she was in the midst of working with a very challenging group. And Mary quickly identified such high levels of acting out behavior as the source for her high level of emotional exhaustion.

Table 9.3 **Results of the Maslach Burnout Inventory**

Burnout	Mary's scores	National normed means (n = +2000)
Emotional exhaustion	24.3	17
Depersonalization	9.2	10
Personal accomplishments	38.9	36

Table 9.4 **Results of the role conflict assessment**

Role conflict	Mary: 1–6 scale	School counselors (n = 200): 1–6 scale
I have to do things that should be done differently	3.5	3.9
I receive an assignment without adequate resources	3.6	3.5
I work with two or more groups who operate differently	3.0	4.5
I receive an assignment without proper human resources	2.9	3.9
I do things that are apt to be accepted by some and not by others	2.9	4.2

3   Results for Mary's role conflict assessment (Table 9.4) indicated that she has less role conflict when compared to school counselors (Coll & Freeman, 1997). However, Mary does indicate elevated role conflict for "doing things that should be done differently" and "receiving an assignment without adequate resources" (+3.0).

Elevated role conflict for "doing things that should be done differently" and "receiving an assignment without adequate resources" are also typical in setting working with the most at-risk youth (Coll & Freeman, 1997). Frank discussions with Mary and her supervisor concerning the specific areas of conflict quickly paid off and Mary was able to streamline certain duties, especially in record keeping and administrative tasks.

Table 9.5 Thriving/distress scores from the MPD

	Mary's score (n = 20)	National norms (n = +1800)
Psychological thriving		
Industry	62%	50%
Generativity	54%	49%
Psychological distress		
Trust	24%	50%
Intimacy	35%	49%
Isolation	62%	49%
Despair	76%	50%

4   In terms of thriving and distress per the MPD (Table 9.5), Mary indicates above-average scores for industry (defined as productivity, seeing a project to the end) and generativity (defined as sharing what you know); however, she indicated much psychological distress in other areas, especially related to trust, intimacy, isolation, and despair.

Mary and I took a more indirect route to deal with improving her low trust and intimacy scores and reducing her isolation and despair scores. We focused on problem solving around creating more support. See below.

• Consultation: It is essential in the helping professional field to prevent isolation and redundancy of ineffective techniques. Mary reported that the coaching with me helped. But perhaps more powerfully, through our discussions, Mary got the idea and created a confidential interdisciplinary youth consultation/support group by collaborating monthly with a teacher, a clergy, a police officer, a judge, and a paraprofessional, all of whom bring specific expertise and appropriate care to the youth mental healthcare area.
• Continuing education: This is another large component to keeping abreast of current issues and trends.

Collaboration with other professionals in the form of an online course brought this needed information to Mary.

- Applying for and receiving a grant: This greatly helped Mary get more support to provide additional services, with more resources.
- Mary also became involved in the training of helping professionals via practicum and internship hours. She is very much enjoying mentoring while getting more help to share the load.

Mary was renewed through these activities and the organization gained from her experiences in that new protocols were introduced concerning record keeping and balancing of youth, especially those scoring +60 with high risk to others across cottages.

Chapter Summary

Helping professionals working with youth often need help themselves in order to remain effective. As we have seen with Mary, specific foci on self-awareness via instruments used here and coaching can make all the difference.

References

Coll, K.M., & Freeman, B. (1997). Role conflict among elementary school counselors: A national comparison with middle and secondary school counselors. *Elementary School Guidance and Counseling, 31*, 251–261.

Coll, K.M., & Haas, R. (2013). Rural adolescent residential treatment facilities as centers of clinical support and excellence. *Advances in Applied Sociology, 3*(2), 102–105.

Coll, K.M., & Rice, R. (1993). Role conflict among community college counselors. *Community College Review, 21*(1), 58–67.

Hawley, G.A. (1987). Measures of psychosocial development (MPD). Retrieved May 15, 2006, from www.ascs4help.com/testing/person-counsel/mpd.htm.

Lyons, J.S., Kisiel, C.L., Dulcan, M., Cohen, R., & Chelser, P. (1997). Crisis assessment and psychiatric hospitalization of children and adolescents in state custody. *Journal of Child and Family Studies, 6*(2), 2–18.

Maslach, C., Jackson, S.E., and Leiter, M.P. (1981). *The Maslach Burnout Inventory* (Research edition). Palo Alto, CA: Consulting Psychologists Press.

McWhirter, J., McWhirter, B., McWhirter, E., & McWhirter, R. (2007). *At risk youth: A comprehensive response for counselors, teachers, psychologists, and human services professionals* (4th ed.). Belmont, CA: Thomson Brooks/Cole.

INDEX

Page numbers in *italics* denote tables.

Made in the USA
Coppell, TX
03 August 2020

32231703R00095